'A wonderful book that w
all that the Lord has for y
and, most importantly, live
Gavin Calver, Director of Mission, Evangelical Alliance

'In these times we desperately need followers of Christ on the front foot of mission leading bold, unashamedly Jesus-centred lives and who make Him known wherever they are; followers who are filled with compassion, courage and a heart for those who don't know Him. This book will light up your heart and stir you to a new level of discipleship.'
Carl Beech, Deputy CEO, The Message Trust

'Certain people seem to carry a unique passion throughout their lives. In *Rouse the Warriors* you will discover this strong heartbeat for prayer, holy living and kingdom advancement. This passion is modelled wonderfully through Steve's family and consistently through the church he leads. His one desire in life is to see followers of Jesus rise up, live cleanly and boldly obey. This is not a theoretical book. It is biblical, practical and possible.'
Stuart Bell, Senior Pastor, Alive Church and Leader of Groundlevel Network

'Steve has done the Body of Christ a great service in writing this excellent and ever-timely book. *Rouse the Warriors* is both inspirational and practical, giving the reader not only vision for what God can do through a life surrendered to Him, but also providing the spiritual tools to rise up from their present state into a life of wholeness, victory and effective service in the Kingdom of God.'
Jonathan Conrathe, Mission24

'Steve Uppal has written a compelling, prophetic cry to the Church to wake up, hear the word of the Lord and go to war. I heartily agree! The souls of nations hang in the balance, and only a prepared, alert and steadfast body of believers can bring their societies the godly transformation so many are desperate for. I encourage you to heed this word, learn from it, pray over it and then boldly obey the Holy Spirit, as the mighty Warrior God created you to!'
Roberts Liardon, Author of God's Generals, Pastor of Embassy Christian Centre, Orlando

'This powerful and timely publication contains one of the most vital messages the Church in this generation needs to hear. The content is as inspirational as it is challenging, and is made all the more pertinent by the fact that its author, writing from long and deep experience, practises everything that he encourages the reader to embrace. If this work was a weapon it should be part of every believer's armoury.'
John Glass, previously General Superintendent, Elim Pentecostal Churches (retired)

'Pastor Steve Uppal carries a gift from God that awakens the Church to a deeper hunger and a greater pursuit of the presence of God. *Rouse the Warriors* not only inspires the reader to hunger for more of God, but it also empowers with a sense of ability to go deeper. Between these covers you'll find both information and impartation to rouse the Warrior that exists in the heart of every believer!'
Lawrence Neisent, Pastor of Destiny Church, Oklahoma City

'In a world that has become increasingly accustomed to conflict and struggle, the ability to keenly discern the nature of the "battle" that is raging, both within and without, is

vitally important to our personal peace and fulfilled purpose. Survival is the first goal in every war, but life was meant for more than surviving. In fact, you were designed to occupy places of divine promise and to thrive in the midst of them. In his book *Rouse The Warriors* Steve has captured the attitude and the aptitude necessary to do just that. As a leader, Steve is gifted with deeply insightful yet simple principles that will "rouse" every person who is sleepwalking through what may be their greatest moments of opportunity. This is a day to advance! To contend for what has been promised. Don't treat this moment or this book casually; your life depends on it!'
Bishop Tony Miller, Pastor of The Gate Church, Oklahoma City and Leader of Destiny Network

'Part of a prophet's message is to awaken the church, to mobilise the church and to bring clarity and focus on how to build its strength. When people are healed, they are not conscious of how great God is in them. This book brings inner healing to realise God's greatness in you. Every time I am with Steve, I receive a new charge of the Holy Spirit. My prayer is that this book will do that for you also.'
Dr Sharon Stone, CI Europe

'*Rouse the Warriors* is a clarion call to the twenty-first-century church. God is raising up an army of devoted, passionate, faith filled followers of Jesus who are ready to respond to His call. My advice would be to not read Steve Uppal's book if you are not prepared to be challenged – it would be best to put it down now and find a more comfortable read. But if you are up for an adventure, even a battle, this could be God's book for you.'
Steve Clifford, General Director, Evangelical Alliance

'This book, *Rouse The Warriors*, is a must read. Steve articulates so well the purpose for which Christ was revealed: that He came to destroy the works of the enemy wherever He went. As we are called to be like Him then we need to wake up to this sense of victory and stop putting up with the enemy, his works and devices. I recommend it to anyone who is wanting to experience victorious living in every aspects of their life, marriage, family, work and church. You will find practical help as well as a great inspirational teaching which will fire you up to make sure that you don't tolerate the enemy any longer and instead experience how God's kingdom is a kingdom of victory and not defeat.

This book will help you not just theologically but also practically to experience victorious living in every aspect of your life. It will inspire you to become intolerant to the devices of the enemy, teach you to be an overcomer in the realisation that greater is He that is in you than he that is in the world, and to discover that God's kingdom is a kingdom of victory and not defeat.'.

David L'Herroux, CEO of United Christian Broadcasters

'*Rouse the Warriors* is my friend Steve Uppal's "life message". Whatever he does, I have always found he stirs the Church to strength, to power, to new possibilities and to defeat the impossible. You can't help but be stronger when you hang around his life and this message he carries. As you read *Rouse the Warriors* the grace of God on Steve's life will impact you powerfully – get ready to rise, to expand, to stand a lot taller in God and to reach a lot further in grace. This is a life-changing, Church-shaping, world-changing book!

Jarrod Cooper, Senior Leader, Revive Church

ROUSE
THE WARRIORS

A PROPHETIC CALL TO ADVANCE THE KINGDOM

STEVE UPPAL

instant
ap◻stle

First published in Great Britain in 2018

Instant Apostle
The Barn
1 Watford House Lane
Watford
Herts
WD17 1BJ

The views and opinions expressed in this work are those of the author and do not necessarily reflect the views and opinions of the publisher.

British Library Cataloguing-in-Publication Data

A catalogue record for this book is available from the British Library

This book and all other Instant Apostle books are available from Instant Apostle:

Website: www.instantapostle.com
E-mail: info@instantapostle.com

ISBN 978-1-909728-86-8

Printed in Great Britain

Dedication

This book is dedicated to the generations of believers who have gone before us, many of whom were not famous or mentioned in the history books. They have faithfully passed the baton to us. Because of their faith, courage and example we are better prepared to run our race. May we run in such a way as to honour them.

To the forgotten heroes ...

Contents

Introduction

Dear Reader

I am so excited to be able to write this book. I believe it is a message that God is speaking to the body of Christ all over the world. It is relevant for every culture, and for young and old alike. I want to encourage you from the start of this book to open up your heart to the Holy Spirit and to allow Him to speak to you through these words. I believe that your life can and will be changed as you read. These are not just words, but truth that can set you free and take you into the next level of your walk with God.

If you read this book for information only, it will not help you. I have not written it as a theological study, but a book from the heart, prompted by the Holy Spirit. I believe it is a prophetic word for the Church. You will need to weigh it and apply it with the balance of other prophetic messages. We 'know in part' (1 Corinthians 13:9) and it is as we put these different parts together that we will understand the whole.

My prayer is that God would use the message in this book to stir many believers into their rightful place in the body of Christ. I also pray that it will help to equip and empower this end-time army for the battles that are ahead of us. I know some in the body are wounded. I feel strongly for them and believe that they are an important part of this army. I trust that the chapter on healing the wounded Warrior (chapter 4) will bring release and wholeness.

In my years of preaching and ministering, I have noticed that we are often better at listening and reading than we are at applying and obeying. The truth in this book will only help you if it is applied and worked out in your life. I believe the Holy Spirit will give grace to apply these truths to all those who ask Him for it.

I would like to make one request. I have quoted quite a few scriptures in this book. I know that some have a habit of skipping the scriptures! Let me urge you to read them. There is power in the Word of God, and it will help greatly in understanding and receiving this message.

Will you take a few moments now to pray and ask God to reveal Himself and His truth to you as you read?

Steve Uppal
Spring 2018

Proclaim – to shout an official announcement in a public place

Passive – sluggish, not active or participating

Rouse – to become active, to wake from sleep, to be excited in thought or action from a state of indolence or inattention

Chapter 1
The Trumpet Call

The vision

A number of years ago, I was invited to preach in a church. During the worship time, the Lord spoke to me through a vision. I could see a very large open space, filled with many people. I knew that the people were believers and represented the Church. They were all involved in various different activities. Some were worshipping the Lord; some were talking to each other; some were standing, some sitting, some isolated and others in groups. There was no real order or purpose to this group of believers; everybody was doing their own thing.

My attention was then drawn to an angel on a hillside overlooking the mass of people. The angel had in his hand a long, straight trumpet. I saw the angel lift the trumpet to his mouth and begin to blow. A strong, loud sound came from the trumpet; it sounded like an alarm, a wake-up call. There were mixed responses to the trumpet call. Some Christians were so engrossed in what they were doing that they didn't even lift their heads. There were others who looked, looked around and then went back to what they were doing before. But there were believers who heard the sound, and responded to it by stopping what they were doing and giving their attention fully to this sound from heaven. Those that had stood to attention stood strong, facing the angel; they were alert, focused and ready for action. For these surrendered Christians, the sound from the trumpet went through them, imparting strength and causing them to grow in stature.

A powerful army

Then, still in the vision, the Lord spoke to me that He was raising a powerful end-time army. I was to be one of many across the earth who have been called to blow a trumpet and rouse this army to attention and action. The Holy Spirit said that if people would respond by opening up their hearts to this message, then the sound of the words would go through them, making them strong and increasing their stature.

The greatest army the world has ever seen is being assembled, made up of men, women and children, people from every tribe, tongue and nation. The educated and uneducated, poor and rich are all responding to the trumpet call. The army is being assembled on every continent of our planet. It is an army greater than our world has ever seen, more powerful than any historical or present-day army. They will be a mighty force for the kingdom of God in these last days.

This army is not armed with physical weapons such as knives, guns or heavy artillery. Their enemy is not an enemy of flesh and blood, or a particular nation on earth. They are armed with spiritual weapons fighting a spiritual enemy. Though the battle is spiritual, the results will be seen clearly in the natural realm. Lives will be changed as individuals encounter Christ. Marriages will be restored, families put back together again and churches will find their rightful, God-given place in our society. No longer will they be apologetic, passive survivors but, instead, radical Kingdom Advancers in their cities, nations and the world. Communities too will be transformed as the army begins its advance.

The world is becoming darker and more evil, but this army will become stronger and its light brighter. It will be a beacon of hope to the lost, and will save many from the dominion of darkness into the kingdom of light. The world has not seen anything like this army before. Some laugh at the Church in its present condition, but the day is coming when they will laugh no more. They will see the Church as a strong force of hope and life in our world. When there is instability and fear all around, they will see stability and safety in the body of Christ.

Prepare for war!

> Proclaim this among the nations: Prepare for war! Rouse the warriors! Let all the fighting men draw near and attack. Beat your ploughshares into swords and your pruning hooks into spears. Let the weakling say, 'I am strong!' Come quickly, all you

nations from every side, and assemble there. Bring
down your warriors, LORD!
Joel 3:9-11

Whether you believe it or not, we are in a war. There is a
battle on right now for the souls of men and women. God
has worked out a great plan of salvation and has given His
only Son that all who believe in Him may have eternal life.
The devil is trying his utmost to keep as many people as he
can from that truth and from salvation. This is a battle for
people's lives and people are precious.

Many in the Church have been passive survivors. The
light of Jesus in most believers has been a dim, flickering
flame. We are busy with our programmes, and trying to
keep our little church worlds alive. We are busy, but busy
with the wrong stuff. Our Christianity has evolved around
our programmed activity and services; these are what we
live for and spend most of our time and money on. Much
of our energy and focus is used up in church politics and
pleasing or appeasing people. There has been much
infighting within the ranks, people trying to preserve their
little kingdoms. While we are busy majoring on minors and
fighting each other, we remain irrelevant to the world
around us and thousands each day slip into a Christ-less
eternity. They know little if anything about what we
believe or even that we exist.

We need to regain an eternal perspective. Many
believers have a temporal or temporary perspective. They
are living for here and now, consumed by material things
and have lost sight of the fact that this life is very short and
we stand on the brink of eternity. I have a painting on my
study wall with a quotation from C T Studd that reads:

Only one life,
Twill soon be past
Only what's done
For Christ will last

We must begin to prepare for war. The trumpet has sounded to rouse the Warriors and wake them from their slumber. Believers and churches must be stirred and woken out of complacency, apathy, blindness, passivity and distraction. They must be brought into a place of being fully awake and ready for action.

It is time to arise from sleep to alertness, from laziness to action, from apathy to expectancy, from hurt to healing, from mediocrity to excellence, from self-pity to gratitude, from failure to success. It is time to leave the past in the past, and take hold of today and the future. It is time to move from a worldly culture to devotion to the kingdom culture, from doubt to faith, from fear to boldness, from limitation to enlargement and from uncertainty to confidence.

Let all the fighting men draw near and attack

The reason the Son of God appeared was to destroy the devil's work.
1 John 3:8

It is time for us to attack the enemy just as Jesus did. The Bible tells us that this was the purpose for which He was revealed. Jesus destroyed the works of the enemy wherever He went. If we are to be like Him, we too must destroy the works of the enemy. Christians have put up with the enemy and his works and devices for too long. Whether it is in our personal lives, marriage, family, work or church, we should not put up with the enemy any longer. We have been conditioned not to fight but to accept the place where we find ourselves. We do not question 'why?' or ask whether the situation could change. It is time for a spiritual fight; you were not just called to defend and hold on to ground, but to attack and advance. Expel the enemy and establish the kingdom of God.

Our lives are not a popularity contest; it is not about being liked or being acceptable. True Christianity has always gone against the grain of popular culture because our values are from above. Too many Christians are always trying to be nice and accepted by people, not appreciating that the truth will offend some. Jesus went against the normal acceptable behaviour of His day; people were offended and upset with Him much of the time. The balance here is that Jesus never offended people because of His personal habits or bad attitude; it was the truth that offended them. Jesus was loyal to the Father and His calling above the culture and religion of the time. We too must be true to biblical culture above our earthly culture, true to the truth of God's Word. You are first Christian and then Indian, English, African, Polish or from any other culture. The greater the freedom you walk in, the more influence you can have in bringing freedom to others.

Beat your ploughshares into swords and your pruning hooks into spears

This passage from Joel talks about turning the tools of farming (maintenance and survival) into weapons of warfare (advancement and invasion). Many have been good at surviving and keeping things at an acceptable level, but have not taken any ground or affected their world for Jesus. We are not called to keep things at an acceptable level, and simply coast through life. Maintenance is good for a season, but you cannot live there or you will die there. We have been maintaining in prayer, vision, planning, evangelism, and even in our personal lives and walk with God. It is time to move out of maintaining to advancing, from surviving to invading.

God has not called you only to hold the fort but to go out from the fort and push the enemy back and take more ground. We should take back what the devil has stolen, and establish the kingdom of God. Advance! It will take courage, boldness, faith and a pioneering spirit to advance, but this generation of Warriors have those qualities, and will advance and pioneer a new way. Though this may be new to us, it is not a new thing. The early disciples lived this way. They were not settlers but pioneers. They were not people-pleasers but God-pleasers. They were not building their own kingdoms but the kingdom of God. They were not serving themselves but serving Jesus. They turned the world upside down in a few short years, advancing the kingdom and destroying the works of the enemy!

Come quickly, all you nations ... and assemble there

And do this, understanding the present time: the hour has already come for you to wake up from your slumber, because our salvation is nearer now than when we first believed. The night is nearly over; the

day is almost here. So let us put aside the deeds of darkness and put on the armour of light.
Romans 13:11-12

We must wake up from our slumber and realise the urgency of the hour in which we are alive. There is a challenge to come quickly, to respond immediately. This call is coming from our Lord and master Jesus, not from an earthly man. Yet in the Church, we have often been slow in our obedience to the Lord. Many have lived with a delusion that they have all the time in the world to obey the Lord. They have the intention that 'one day' they will do what needs to be done. But one day never comes. It is always sometime in the future.

I recently challenged one of the people in my church about their commitment and obedience to the Lord. The Lord was asking certain things from this individual in lifestyle changes, and there was a challenge for them to walk in their calling. This challenge had been going on for a number of years. Their response shocked me. They said they were not worried about it, and that it would all work out in the end. So many are deluded and have a false sense of security. Walking in disobedience is a dangerous thing. It results in many wasted years that could have been filled with productivity for the kingdom. Today is the day you need to respond to the prompting and voice of the Holy Spirit.

So, as the Holy Spirit says:
'Today, if you hear his voice, do not harden your hearts as you did in the rebellion.'
Hebrews 3:7-8

We need to move with the Lord as He leads, and change when He shows us what needs to be changed. Many take the grace of God in vain, thinking that they can just do what they like when they like and God understands. They fail to understand that grace enables us to live godly lives in and keep in step with the Spirit. Grace teaches us to say no to ungodliness and yes to a godly life. God expects obedience from his children. Yes, He is patient with us and a loving father, but Proverbs 29:1 tells me that 'whoever remains stiff-necked after many rebukes will suddenly be destroyed – without remedy'! You have to decide to do something about the apathy and the complacency in your life. This army will also be correctly assembled. There will be no jostling or taking another's place. Each will know their place and stay in their place. They will realise that being in the right place brings greater fruitfulness for them and allows them to be a blessing to all around them. Some have wanted other people's roles or jobs and caused much trouble and striving in their own flesh to get them. Stop struggling and striving, manipulating situations and people; move to where the Lord has put you.

The first step is always one of surrender. 'Not my will, but yours be done' (Luke 22:42). I believe the fastest way to get God's attention and become fruitful in the kingdom is to surrender yourself to Him. Give Him wholehearted devotion. As the apostle Paul said:

> I have been crucified with Christ and I no longer live, but Christ lives in me. The life I live in the body, I live by faith in the Son of God, who loved me and gave himself for me.
> *Galatians 2:20*

The trumpet has sounded... The call has gone out... The Holy Spirit is speaking to you. Will you join this end-time army of Warriors? You now have a responsibility to respond to the challenge of this chapter. Maintain or advance? Survive or invade new ground? Live for the temporal or live for eternity? The choice is yours.

Application

- In which areas of your life do you feel like you have settled into maintaining?

- Are you willing to change?

- Take thirty minutes today with Bible, pen and paper, and prayerfully write down what you need to do to change.

- Pray through these areas, committing them to the Lord and asking for His help.

Commission – empower with a commission, give authority, entrust with an office or duty, and prepare for active service

Advance – forward motion, progression, a step forward

Demonstrate – make known by outward indications

Chapter 2
Kingdom Advancers Commissioned

Regaining the importance of the Great Commission

The purpose of this army is clearly outlined in Scripture.

> Then Jesus came to them and said, 'All authority in heaven and on earth has been given to me. Therefore go and make disciples of all nations, baptising them in the name of the Father and of the Son and of the Holy Spirit, and teaching them to obey everything I have commanded you. And surely I am with you always, to the very end of the age.'
> *Matthew 28:18-20*

This passage of Scripture has been forgotten by some, made little of by others, and ignored by many believers. It is difficult to misunderstand, because it is so straightforward and simple. We need to give these words of Jesus priority in our lives and churches. They need to be at the core of our thinking and planning. These are not the words of a man, but the words of the Lord Jesus Christ, the Son of God, our Saviour. They were some of the last words Jesus spoke before He left the earth, so they are very important. They are not only spoken to the disciples of Jesus' day, but to every believer that professes faith in Jesus Christ. It is not the great suggestion, or an optional extra, but it is the Great Commission of Jesus, and it is for you and for me.

This is it:

- All authority in heaven and on earth has been given to me [Jesus].

- Go and make disciples of all nations,

- Baptising them ...

- Teaching them to obey everything ...

- I am with you always ...

This is for all believers, not just for those in ministry or those called 'evangelist'. Millions are going to an eternity without Jesus and, unless you and I tell them about Christ, they will be lost. There is no greater work to be involved in, or greater duty to be discharged. Not only is it our duty as believers to fulfil this desire and commission of Jesus, but I believe it is a privilege to share the good news of Jesus Christ with those who are lost.

God loves the lost

> For God so loved the world that he gave his one and
> only Son, that whoever believes in him shall not
> perish but have eternal life.
> *John 3:16*

God still loves the world; His heart still beats for those who
don't know Him. He loved the world enough to send His
one and only son to die for them; He then entrusted the
great message of salvation to His Church, to you and to me.
We are His hands, His feet and His mouth on this earth.
Will you personally accept the Great Commission of Jesus?
Will you make it your responsibility? Do you love the lost
like He does? Will you give your life to reach those all
around you who are blindly headed for hell? May God
deliver us from our selfish, inward-looking ways.

This end-time army will be burning with a passion for
the lost. They will have the heart of the Father for those
they are surrounded by. A heart that burns with passion
for people. A heart that is committed to tell others the
words of eternal life. A heart that rejoices over one who
receives Christ more than in great wealth. These Warriors
will pray and weep for the lost and obey Jesus' commission
and go to them with the words of salvation. They will be
Kingdom Advancers, advancing the kingdom of God
wherever they go.

Early Kingdom Advancers

> After this the Lord appointed seventy-two others
> and sent them two by two ahead of him to every
> town and place where he was about to go. He told

them, 'The harvest is plentiful, but the workers are few. Ask the Lord of the harvest, therefore, to send out workers into his harvest field. Go! I am sending you out like lambs among wolves.'
Luke 10:1-3

Jesus was equipping His followers to follow Him in what He was doing. He sent out others to work with Him advancing the kingdom. They preached the good news of the kingdom and challenged people to repent. They healed the sick, and cast out demons. They were destroying all the works of the enemy and establishing the kingdom of God. We too have this same calling upon our lives.

The ultimate Kingdom Advancer

… how God anointed Jesus of Nazareth with the Holy Spirit and power, and how he went around doing good and healing all who were under the power of the devil, because God was with him.
Acts 10:38

Jesus is our greatest example, and we see that He spent His earthly life destroying the works of the enemy and advancing the kingdom of God. You need to do the same works that Jesus did. You are now His disciple called to take His message to the ends of the earth. You are invited into the mission of God to destroy the works of the enemy in your family, city and nation. Not only to destroy the works of the enemy, but also to establish the kingdom of God. You are destined to bring light into dark situations, hope to the hopeless. God created you to give courage to the discouraged and life to those who are dead.

An army of Kingdom Advancers is already marching through our world doing the work of their Saviour, Jesus; I encourage you to join them. Move from passivity and conformity to righteous, bold action for the kingdom. This is what you were born for.

Four ways to advance the kingdom

1. Be a kingdom person

Live the life and be a kingdom person. We have many believers trying to live out a formula that they have been taught, but their hearts have not been transformed. They are trying to change the outward actions without changing the thought patterns and attitudes on the inside. We often do this with our churches; we have believers who know the protocol in church, how they should behave, what they should say and how they should dress. We end up with a Church that looks good but often has little or no power. We must change the thoughts and attitudes of the person and not look at the outward appearances.

> Therefore, if anyone is in Christ, the new creation has come: the old has gone, the new is here!
> *2 Corinthians 5:17*

If you are a believer in Christ, the old has gone and the new has come. You have a new nature. You have Christ living inside you. You don't have to live by your strength alone, but Christ imparts His heavenly nature to you through the power of His work on the cross. Stop trying to live by rules, regulations and dos and don'ts. Live by His power in you. It is 'Christ in you, the hope of glory'

(Colossians 1:27). Walk in relationship with Him daily by talking and listening to Him. In John 15 Jesus invites us into an intimate, abiding relationship with Himself. It's in that relationally connected place that we 'become'; He transforms and changes us by His love and power.

Who you are is far more important than what you do. What you do will flow out from who you are. You are called a human being, not a human doing. Conduct always flows out from character, so when we change the character the conduct will automatically change. Feeding on God's Word, the Bible, will teach you what a kingdom person looks like. You need to allow the Word to wash your attitudes and ways of thinking, therefore, renewing your mind. Paul said it this way:

> Do not conform any longer to the pattern of this world, but be transformed by the renewing of your mind. Then you will be able to test and approve what God's will is – his good, pleasing and perfect will.
> *Romans 12:2*

Read the Gospels and study the life of Jesus; you are called to be like Him. Ask the Holy Spirit to change you to become a kingdom person. The way to change on the inside is to feed on the Bible and seek the Spirit's help to apply it to your life. We will look at these things in greater depth in the coming chapters. Let me encourage you to be a kingdom person. You are a citizen of the kingdom of God. If that truth gets on the inside of you, it will transform you and the world around you.

Kingdom people will be Kingdom Advancers wherever they are. They will not be trying to do the right thing or force something. They have a living, intimate relationship with Jesus that causes the power of God to live in them and flow through them to those around. You are not to be a thermometer that reflects the temperature, but a thermostat that sets the temperature.

2. Preach (or speak) the good news

> How, then, can they call on the one they have not believed in? And how can they believe in the one of whom they have not heard? And how can they hear without someone preaching to them?
> *Romans 10:14*

I have never seen a Bible jump up, run down the street, and declare the wonders of God. God has chosen to use people to speak the good news. Unless you and I speak the truth about Christ and His great work of salvation, unbelievers will remain ignorant of the gospel. We are called to speak out the life-giving message and share it with others. I have heard some say, 'Let your life be a witness; you don't need to speak the gospel, just live it.' There is a truth in that; we do need to let our lives be shining lights to others, but the gospel still needs to be spoken. An unspoken gospel is no gospel at all.

> For when I preach the gospel, I cannot boast, since I am compelled to preach. Woe to me if I do not preach the gospel!
> *1 Corinthians 9:16*

This is the cry of a kingdom man whose heart has been captured by the Saviour. These words need to become our words and our heartbeat. We too need to be compelled to speak the good news of Jesus Christ and His saving power. You may speak to one or two in a shop or on the street. You may speak to a room full of relatives. You may speak before a hall full of schoolchildren. You may stand before hundreds or thousands and speak. However, you must speak, whether to many or to few. As the Lord opens doors and opportunities, then seize them and preach the good news of Jesus' saving power!

The Church has been quiet for too long. Some have been afraid to speak the truth for fear of rejection, ridicule or persecution. Our world today is a challenging and complex place to live out one's faith boldly. There are increasing stories of people being taken to court or losing their employment for living out their faith. I don't think it was too different for the apostle Paul and the Early Church. We need to walk wisely, understanding the culture of our day and yet not allowing ourselves to be muted.[1]

> The gospel of Christ does not move by popular waves. It has no self-propagating power. It moves as the men who have charge of it move.
> *E M Bounds*[2]

---

[1] The Evangelical Alliances Resource 'Speak Up' is very helpful in understanding our religious freedoms and will give you clarity and confidence. http://www.eauk.org/current-affairs/politics/speak-up.cfm (accessed 23rd January 2018).

[2] https://www.ccel.org/ccel/bounds/power.I_1.html (accessed 23rd January 2018).

3. Do good deeds

Then he will say to those on his left, 'Depart from me, you who are cursed, into the eternal fire prepared for the devil and his angels. For I was hungry and you gave me nothing to eat, I was thirsty and you gave me nothing to drink, I was a stranger and you did not invite me in, I needed clothes and you did not clothe me, I was ill and in prison and you did not look after me.'

They also will answer, 'Lord, when did we see you hungry or thirsty or a stranger or needing clothes or ill or in prison, and did not help you?' He will reply, 'Truly I tell you, whatever you did not do for one of the least of these, you did not do for me.'

Then they will go away to eternal punishment, but the righteous to eternal life.
Matthew 25:41-46

You are the salt of the earth. But if the salt loses its saltiness, how can it be made salty again? It is no longer good for anything, except to be thrown out and trampled underfoot.

You are the light of the world. A town on a hill cannot be hidden. Neither do people light a lamp and put it under a bowl. Instead they put it on its stand, and it gives light to everyone in the house. In the same way, let your light shine before others, that they may see your good deeds and glorify your Father in heaven.
Matthew 5:13-16

These two passages speak for themselves. Again, let me remind you that these are the words of Jesus Christ. Jesus gives us a strong challenge here. We must meet the needs of the needy in our communities. The hungry, thirsty, strangers, naked, prisoners, the sick and the poor are our responsibility as believers. It has been encouraging to see the Church increase in its social outreach in recent times, but there is still much room for improvement and more churches need to be involved. The poor and marginalised are on the heart of God, and they must be on our hearts too. They cannot be ignored, and must not be forgotten.

I remember listening to a preacher sharing a team experience many years ago in Russia. They were involved in holding meetings and smuggling Bibles into the country. One day, they were filming the terrible poverty of a bread line. People had queued for hours to buy a loaf of bread. The van came and delivered the bread to the shop. There was not enough, and most of the people went away hungry. As the preacher and his team were filming the situation, a lady asked the interpreter what they were doing. He proudly told her that they were bringing the Word of God into their country. The lady replied, 'Tell them that their Bibles don't fill our empty stomachs.'

We need to meet the physical needs of those around us if we are to be effective in preaching Christ. Some have been so busy building their nice churches and their nice lives that they have no place in their lives for the needy of our world. Read the words of Jesus above, and see how strongly He feels about this. He says that when we meet their needs, we are meeting His needs. He identifies with the poor, broken, lonely and outcast.

People will see your good deeds, and then they may turn to God themselves and praise Him. It will not be our religious fervour or our long prayers that will shine hope to the world, but our acts of kindness for the hurting. Become a Kingdom Advancer by the good deeds you do for the hurting, needy and forgotten of our world. The Church should lead the way in social care.

4. Demonstrate the power of the gospel

He said to them, 'Go into all the world and preach the gospel to all creation. Whoever believes and is baptised will be saved, but whoever does not believe will be condemned. And these signs will accompany those who believe: in my name they will drive out demons; they will speak in new tongues; they will pick up snakes with their hands; and when they drink deadly poison, it will not hurt them at all; they will place their hands on people who are ill, and they will get well.'
Mark 16:15-18

There is power in the name of Jesus. Believers ought to be demonstrating that power in their daily lives. Many have allowed fear or wrong teaching to stop them from operating in the power of God. Many of our churches have been void of God's power. Therefore, we have a generation of believers who are conditioned not to expect demonstrations of God's power. Hebrews 13:8 tells us that Jesus is the same yesterday, today, and for ever. His desires, His power and His abilities are still the same. Jesus does heal the sick, and He wants to heal them through you.

He can also give you words of wisdom or knowledge about a person.

These things are not just for our public meetings, but they are to be an integral part of our everyday lives. In the home or the workplace or out shopping, Jesus lives in you, and wants to demonstrate His power through you. Ask God to grant you opportunities to demonstrate His power, and when the opportunities come, have the courage and faith to seize them. A key characteristic of this army will be that the power of their Christianity will be demonstrated in everyday life.

It may be as simple as praying with a colleague at work who is suffering from a headache. It might be quietly asking God for wisdom when a friend shares their problems with you. Do not be afraid then to share what the Spirit prompts you with! A friend may share an issue concerning their son, and you offer to pray that God will turn the situation around. Do not be embarrassed to pray in public with unbelievers. Always be polite and sensitive and ask if they would like you to pray. I believe God honours these prayers, and the unbeliever is touched by your love and concern for them. God loves those who do not yet know him, and is looking for opportunities to show Himself to them.

We have been entrusted with the most important and valuable message in the world. A whole army is being roused to carry this message and advance the kingdom across the world. Will you become a Kingdom Advancer today?

From the days of John the Baptist until now, the kingdom of heaven has been forcefully advancing, and forceful men lay hold of it.
Matthew 11:12 (NIV 1984)

Application

- Meditate on the words from Matthew 28:18-20.

- How will you obey these words of Jesus?

- What lifestyle changes will be needed to do the following four things?

  1. Be a kingdom person
  2. Preach (or speak) the good news
  3. Do good deeds
  4. Demonstrate the power of the gospel

- Ask the Holy Spirit for wisdom and grace to fulfil the Great Commission.

Authority – power or right to enforce obedience

Power – ability and capacity, control or authority over others, ability to act or affect something strongly

Empower – invest formally with power, authorise, endow with the ability required for a purpose or task

Chapter 3
Kingdom Advancers
Empowered

Commissioned and empowered

> Then Jesus came to them and said, 'All authority in heaven and on earth has been given to me ... And surely I am with you always, to the very end of the age.'
> *Matthew 28:18, 20*

Not only has Jesus given us the Great Commission but He has also empowered us to fulfil that commission. He is a good God, and He always provides what we need to do the task ahead of us. Yes, He has given us a strong charge, a tremendous job to complete, but He has empowered us with the authority we need to complete that job. Through the cross and His shed blood, He bought back all that was lost by Adam. When He spoke to His disciples in Matthew 28:18-20, He started by making a statement that all authority had been given to Him, and finished by saying that He would be always with us. So if He has all authority, and He lives in us and will never leave us, we have authority as we remain in Him and He in us.

Translated from the dominion of darkness into the kingdom of God

> For he has rescued us from the dominion of darkness and brought us into the kingdom of the Son he loves.
> *Colossians 1:13*

Every person is born into the dominion of darkness. They have the devil as their father. He has influence over their lives. He is called the god of this world who blinds the eyes of unbelievers (see 2 Corinthians 4:4). When a person is born again, they are then bought out of the dominion of darkness into the kingdom of God. There is a positional change. They are no longer under the influence of the devil. Though a person can still be tempted, the devil has no legal right over them. They are now in a new kingdom, with new rights and privileges. They are called sons and daughters of God. They have a tremendous inheritance. They have been given authority over all the works of the enemy.

Destroyed by lack of knowledge

> My people are destroyed from lack of knowledge.
> *Hosea 4:6*

The problem has not been in their position, power or authority, but in their lack of knowledge concerning these provisions that are the inheritance and right of every believer. People have been destroyed because of their lack of knowledge. Many Christians live far under their God-ordained place because they are unaware of who they are and what rights they have, and the power available to them. This end-time army will walk in their God-given, blood-bought authority.

I heard the story[3] a long time ago of a lady at the turn of the last century who was dying from starvation and malnutrition; she lived in poverty and squalor. The famous preacher Charles Spurgeon went to visit her. He noticed on the wall above her bed a frame with a piece of paper in it, and he asked the lady where she had acquired this piece of paper. She told him that she had worked many years for a very wealthy mistress. When this mistress was about to die she had given her this piece of paper. The lady was unable to read, but as she had been very close to her mistress, she had a frame made and stuck that piece of paper in it. She had treasured it. It turned out that piece of paper was the will of that mistress. She had left her entire estate and fortune to this poor woman. This woman's lack of knowledge and her inability to read had caused her to live out the rest of her life in poverty.

Many Christians are like that. Jesus has provided a great salvation for us with benefits and provisions, but so many Christians are ignorant of what the Word says. They like the Bible, and hold it in high regard, but they are unaware of what is contained within its pages. Therefore, the enemy lies to them, and steals from them. Christians complain and get upset at their lives and circumstances, but they never rise up and exercise their God-given rights.

---

[3] Source unknown.

It is time for this end-time army to rise up and understand their position in Jesus, and to enforce the defeat of the enemy and the victory of the cross. You can walk in your authority as a believer.

Seated with Christ

I pray also that the eyes of your heart may be enlightened in order that you may know the hope to which he has called you, the riches of his glorious inheritance in the saints, and his incomparably great power for us who believe. That power is like the working of his mighty strength, which he exerted in Christ when he raised him from the dead and seated him at his right hand in the heavenly realms, far above all rule and authority, power and dominion, and every title that can be given, not only in the present age but also in the one to come. And God placed all things under his feet and appointed him to be head over everything for the church, which is his body, the fullness of him who fills everything in every way.
Ephesians 1:18-23 (NIV 1984)

This apostolic prayer is one of my favourite prayers to pray and is a powerful scripture. Please read it again, taking time to stop and digest what it is saying. The apostle Paul is saying to the church in Ephesus that he prays that their spiritual eyes would be opened for them to see three things:

- The hope to which they have been called;

- The riches of his glorious inheritance in the saints ;

- The great power available *for those who believe*.

You can have eyes that see but a heart that is blind to the revelations and truths of God's Word. You need the Holy Spirit to open your spiritual eyes to see these things. I pray this scripture most days for myself, family and the Church. The last third thing he prays for is that they may know 'his incomparably great power for us who believe'. For who? 'For us who believe'. Are you a believer? Then this incomparable power is available to you! Wow! The awesome power that raised Jesus from the dead, then placed Him into the highest position, and gave Him authority above all things. Notice He is seated far above all:

- Rule;

- Authority;

- Power;

- Dominion;

- Every title that can be given;

- Not only in the present age, but also in the one to come.

'God placed all things under [Jesus'] feet and appointed him to be head over everything for the church … his body.' Here is the really exciting bit. He is the head, and we are the body. You are His body, and therefore you have authority like Jesus has, as long as you remain in Him, and

He remains in you. You have authority over all the works of the enemy, in your life, your family, your church, your city/town/village and the world.

Authority

> I have given you authority to trample on snakes and scorpions and to overcome all the power of the enemy; nothing will harm you.
> *Luke 10:19*

Authority has been given to you by Jesus to fulfil the Great Commission He left us. Authority simply means the right to command, to enforce rules, or give orders, holder of power, official permission to act on behalf of someone else.[4] This authority is for every believer who is seeking to fulfil the Great Commission. It is also over all the power of the enemy. He cannot hurt you, but you can hurt him, and break his power over people's lives or communities, even nations. You have been granted official permission and power to do what Jesus has called you to do. Jesus said:

> … whoever believes in me will do the works I have been doing, and they will do even greater things than these, because I am going to the Father.
> *John 14:12*

---

[4] In this book I have based definitions mainly on the Oxford dictionary, but have paraphrased.

The name of Jesus

> In my name they will …
> *Mark 16:17*

> And I will do whatever you ask in my name, so that
> the Father may be glorified in the Son. You may ask
> me for anything in my name, and I will do it.
> *John 14:13-14*

It is in the name of Jesus you have the power to defeat the
enemy. When you speak in His name, the forces of heaven
are right there to enforce what you have spoken. Every
believer has the right to use the name of Jesus. Do not live
in ignorance any longer; take these scriptures, meditate on
them, allow the truth to drop into your heart, and start
walking in your God-given authority. Become a Kingdom
Advancer, destroying the works of the enemy and
establishing the kingdom of God. You have been
empowered. Learn to pray in His name. There is power in
that name when it used by a believer. It is the name above
every name and every tongue will confess and every knee
bow to that name (see Philippians 2:9-11).

The blood

> They overcame him by the blood of the Lamb and by
> the word of their testimony; they did not love their
> lives so much as to shrink from death.
> *Revelation 12:11 (NIV 1984)*

Learn to use the blood. Remind the enemy of what happened at the cross; he was defeated and made a spectacle. A divine exchange took place concerning your life. All your rubbish and sin was exchanged for the righteousness of Christ (see 2 Corinthians 5:17). Speak your testimony, what God has done for you. The enemy hates that. You overcome him by rehearsing and confessing the word of your testimony. Talk to people, talk to God and talk to yourself about what He has done. This stirs faith and thankfulness. The divine exchange is the gospel, it is Christianity, it is humans filled with God's life again – and it is all because of the blood of Jesus. The pure, spotless son of God shed His blood to pay the price for our sin and reconcile us to God.

The purpose of being empowered

We must remember that the purpose of being empowered is to fulfil the Great Commission. It is not just for you, your success, pleasure and provision in this world. Too many selfish believers are trying to work these things for themselves. Jesus' reason for coming to this world and going through with the cross was the salvation of the human race. You are empowered to rescue these precious ones from the clutches of the enemy.

Stay close to Jesus, live in Him, and allow Him to live in you strongly. Build intimacy, get to know Him well, and how He operates. You have authority to the degree the King lives in you. The enemy is not afraid of you, but Christ in you. The enemy recognises when someone is living the life, and has integrity in their walk. James tells us in his first chapter that double-minded people will not 'receive anything from the Lord' (see verses 6-8). You cannot live like a hypocrite, and expect power to flow.

> You, dear children, are from God and have overcome them, because the one who is in you is greater than the one who is in the world.
> *1 John 4:4*

Remember, the greater one, Jesus, lives in you. There is no need to fear or be apprehensive. Walk tall with confidence in Him. Let the Warrior be roused in you and become a Kingdom Advancer in this end-time army.

Application

- Go through the scriptures in this passage, meditate on them, and pray them. They will then become a part of you helping you to walk in your God-given authority.

- Ask the Holy Spirit to teach you how you can live as an overcomer in everyday life.

- Living like Jesus is your goal; He is your supreme example.

Heal – free a person from disease, restore to health

Forgive – pardon an offence, give up resentment against a person, to loose or release

Wound – to cause a wound in the body of somebody, a lasting emotional or psychological injury

Chapter 4
Healing the Wounded Warriors

Wounds do come in times of battle

> For we wrestle not against flesh and blood, but against principalities, against powers, against the rulers of the darkness of this world, against spiritual wickedness in high places.
> *Ephesians 6:12 (KJV)*

> Fight the good fight of the faith. Take hold of the eternal life to which you were called when you made your good confession in the presence of many witnesses.
> *1 Timothy 6:12*

Whether we like it or not we are in a battle, and in times of battle, people can be injured and get hurt. Therefore we need to live diligently and aware at all times. The important things a Warrior needs to learn are first, how to minimise injury, and second, how to heal any wounds as quickly as possible. Not all wounds or injuries have to happen; many could be avoided and deflected by an experienced Warrior. In the same way for us as believers there are many things that we go through, and much pain that we feel that is unnecessary and sometimes even of our own making.

We need the wounded Warriors

I have been involved in Church leadership for more than twenty-five years and my observation is that there are many wounded Warriors in the body of Christ today. These wounded Warriors are an important part of this end-time army, and they cannot be overlooked, or their importance underestimated. These Warriors have great potential to fight in the army of the Lord. They have wisdom, understanding, experience and love, and through their wounds being healed, they can bring healing to many others. We need our wounded Warriors. They need to be made whole, so that they can operate in a place of productivity and fruitfulness.

In their wounded state, they carry hurt and disease, and can infect others with their unhealed wounds. Because of this, they have at times been overlooked, ignored and bypassed. Some wounded Warriors have been subjected to further wounds from the body of Christ, mostly due to misunderstanding. We cannot afford to mistreat our wounded, but instead help them to get whole.

I believe that the Lord is giving grace to many of the wounded in order to bring them into a place of healing and wholeness. They need love, support and help from the rest of the body of Christ. Yes, there is a risk of being hurt if you try to get close to a wounded person. Often wounded people are full of pain and scared of being wounded again, and the only defence they know is to hurt others. For example, an injured animal will lash out at a vet who is trying to help it. Vets do not get angry and walk away from the injured animal. They understand the pain, isolation and confusion that the injured animal feels, and will continue to minister healing, even at the risk of personal injury or harm. We must do the same. Minister healing to those who are wounded at the risk of being wounded. Understand that the actions of the hurt person are motivated by pain and confusion. For those of you that are wounded, you must learn to trust the people trying to help you. Do not push them away or lash out at them. Allow their love and words of truth to cleanse, and bring healing to your wounds. It will be painful as your wound is touched and washed, but you must go through that pain if healing and wholeness are to come.

How the enemy works

The enemy uses various means to wound believers. This might be through unfair circumstances, other believers, church politics, unfulfilled dreams or expectations and demonic attacks. It is through these things that there is the potential for offence. Discouragement, unforgiveness, anger, bitterness, resentment, self-pity, jealousy or accusation can come into the Warrior's life. Once the wound is inflicted, it must be treated immediately. If the wound is left untreated then the door is open for further infection. Although you may have been wounded by one specific dart of the enemy, many other weapons can now be used. An open, untreated wound will weaken the Warrior, bringing confusion and disorientation. It will also open the door for other wounds to be inflicted, as your defences will be lowered.

For example, you may have been through a situation where your hopes and desires are left unfulfilled; you had hoped for more, perhaps even been promised more. Disappointment came in, which led to discouragement that led to bitterness. Slowly over the months, you lose your hope and stop trusting God and people. You withdraw from those whom you love. You may even begin to blame others for what happened, and accusation comes into your life. In this condition, you can no longer see clearly. You interpret everything through the eyes of hurt and bitterness. You start to find that you are now beginning to hurt others. Your words have become sharper and cut; you blame and accuse quickly. It started by simply thinking these things, but it has now moved from thoughts to actions. The wounded Warrior is now wounding others, and the reason for this is simple – hurt people hurt people. The only remedy is to visit the wounded area, and minister healing. It will be painful, and it will hurt when someone touches that wound, but it needs cleansing, washing and dressing for healing to come.

Some start on the process to healing, but the pain of visiting those old memories and dealing with wrong attitudes is too much for them, and so they withdraw. They find it too difficult to expose their wounds to the one ministering healing; it is embarrassing to show nakedness. It will take trust and vulnerability for healing to be ministered. It is time for you to be mature and realise that God has not created you to be an island. You are a part of the body and He works through His body. Everything God wants to get to you He does so through relationships.

It may be that someone whom you trusted and loved mistreated you. They betrayed your trust, and let you down. They did or said things that you never thought they could. They should have known better; how could they do this to you after all you had been through together? You were deeply wounded, and you felt that you could never trust anyone again. Just the thought of that person or the mention of their name now causes so much inner pain and anger. You learn to withdraw from people. You build walls around yourself, promising it will never happen again. You learn to live in isolation. Yes, you meet others, and talk to them, but there is a point that you will not go beyond. There is a wound that is still open, daily becoming more infected. Do not carry the pain any more; do not allow the anger to continue. This wound has limited too many relationships. It has stopped you flowing in your God-given destiny. It is time to be healed, to get back in the army and rejoin the fight. God will grant you grace, and He will help you into a place of healing.

Bad things do happen to people who don't deserve it: that is a part of life. We must learn how to deal with those things that happen to us. It is not what happens to you in life that determines your destiny, but how you handle what happens to you. We have all had the opportunity to be offended, or to hold on to unforgiveness, but we must choose to overlook offence, and to forgive the offender.

> See to it that no one falls short of the grace of God and that no bitter root grows up to cause trouble and defile many.
> *Hebrews 12:15*

Friendly fire

In recent wars, it has been amazing to see the high casualties resulting from so-called friendly fire. I believe that this may be something that happens in the Church for as long as we are on earth, but we do need to minimise these wounds. We need to be careful how we treat one another, and not give the enemy an opportunity to come in. We must be wise, and learn from experience and history, so that we do not repeat the mistakes that have been made before. Our natural armies would be foolish indeed if they did not learn from their mistakes from one war to another. The Church too must learn from the past and not keep repeating it.

I firmly believe that there are very few malicious believers. Many people wound or hurt others because they are wounded or immature themselves, or they did not think about what they were doing. It is time for the body of Christ to grow into a new level of maturity. We must stop being offended with one another, and separating from each other.

We must keep the unity of the faith. We have one God, one faith, and we belong to one body. There are too many people building their own empires, and fighting others in an effort to preserve their lot. We must come to the place where we are willing to lay down our lives for each other, and for the advancement of the kingdom. Jesus said, 'Greater love has no one than this: to lay down one's life for one's friends' (John 15:13).

Minimising injury

Finally, be strong in the Lord and in his mighty power. Put on the full armour of God so that you can take your stand against the devil's schemes. For our struggle is not against flesh and blood, but against the rulers, against the authorities, against the powers of this dark world and against the spiritual forces of evil in the heavenly realms. Therefore, put on the full armour of God, so that when the day of evil comes, you may be able to stand your ground, and after you have done everything, to stand. Stand firm then, with the belt of truth buckled around your waist, with the breastplate of righteousness in place, and with your feet fitted with the readiness that comes from the gospel of peace. In addition to all this, take up the shield of faith, with which you can extinguish all the flaming arrows of the evil one. Take the helmet of salvation and the sword of the Spirit, which is the word of God. And pray in the Spirit on all occasions with all kinds of prayers and requests. With this in mind, be alert and always keep on praying for all the Lord's people.
Ephesians 6:10-18

I believe that it is possible for this end-time army to minimise the wounds and injuries they receive. You can grow in wisdom and understanding. If you apply what you learn you will become an experienced soldier, one who is skilled and is not easily wounded. You can minimise the risk of injury by doing the following:

1. Be strong in the Lord

Remember, your strength and confidence does not come from yourself but from Christ. Put your confidence in Him, in His promises, and in His Word. You must learn to keep your relationship with Him alive at all times, both in the good as well as in the tough times. He is the vine and we are the branches. Our strength flows from Him, therefore we must live in Him and He in us.

> Remain in me, and I will remain in you. No branch can bear fruit by itself; it must remain in the vine. Neither can you bear fruit unless you remain in me.
> *John 15:4, NIV 1984*

This must be a daily decision we make to stay connected and dependent upon Him. It is so easy for pride to come in and for us to start drawing strength from our success and achievements. Keep your heart humble and remind yourself that you are who you are because of Jesus. You are protected as you live in Him. The great protection psalm, Psalm 91, is conditional to the believer staying in God. The promises are made to those who dwell 'in the shelter of the Most High'.

He who dwells in the shelter of the Most High will rest in the shadow of the Almighty. I will say of the LORD, 'He is my refuge and my fortress, my God, in whom I trust.'
Psalm 91:1-2 (NIV 1984)

2. *Put on the full armour of God*

The apostle Paul reminds us, in Ephesians 6, of the battle in which we are engaged. He encourages us to 'put on the full armour of God', so that we can take our stand against the schemes of the enemy. The Lord has provided all that we need to stand against the enemy and fight. Armour and weapons are useless unless they are worn and used. Many Christians do not wear their armour or use their weapons against the enemy and, because of this, they receive unnecessary injuries. They treat their armour with contempt, failing to understand its importance for them.

Look again at Ephesians 6:14-17. Truth, righteousness, peace, faith, salvation and God's Word are all given to you to help you fight. You must learn to apply these things to your life. They are more than just words, they are the very things that will protect you from the schemes of the enemy. You must put them on, and practise using them daily. Live in the truth of God's Word, and allow only truth to come from your mouth. Remember that you are righteous because of the work of Jesus on Calvary. Make sure that your actions and lifestyle are righteous each day.

Learn to handle the sword of the Spirit, which is the Word of God. Jesus fought the devil with the Word when He was tempted. You too will need to know the Word well in order to use it against the enemy. Faith is your shield; lift it up, and the enemy's arrows will bounce off your shield. These two (the Word and faith) are very powerful weapons. You must be careful not to lay them down, but keep them in your hands all the time. Become familiar in handling both the sword and the shield.

3. Stay self-controlled and alert

> Be self-controlled and alert. Your enemy the devil prowls around like a roaring lion looking for someone to devour. Resist him, standing firm in the faith, because you know that your brothers throughout the world are undergoing the same kind of sufferings.
> 1 Peter 5:8-9 (NIV 1984)

As an end-time Warrior, you need to be self-controlled. Many lack self-control. They allow themselves to think, speak and do whatever they feel like. They are led by their emotions rather than leading their emotions. This will get you into trouble and open a door for the enemy to attack. This is a major problem in our world today, as many have cast off all restraint (see Proverbs 29:18). They believe in doing whatever they want to do. Sadly, this thinking has come into the lives of many in the Church. Proverbs 25:28 says, 'Like a city whose walls are broken through is a person who lacks self-control.' In other words, when the defences are down, the enemy can easily get in. Learn to exercise self-control in your life. It is one of the fruits of the Spirit that is in you as a believer (see Galatians 5:22-23), and it will help you resist the enemy. Be controlled in what you think, say and do. Don't react to things all the time; hold steady, be still, ask for wisdom.

You also need to be alert, sharp and ready. You cannot be caught slumbering, or off-guard. These self-controlled Warriors will live ready, expectant, and sensitive to the Lord and to their environment. The slightest change in the atmosphere and they will sense it and resist the enemy. We need alert believers, not dull, insensitive ones. Much of our world's pleasures and pampering of the flesh dulls the senses of believers. Stay alert!

4. Walk in obedience

> Then the LORD said to Cain, 'Why are you angry? Why is your face downcast? If you do what is right, will you not be accepted? But if you do not do what is right, sin is crouching at your door; it desires to have you, but you must master it.'
> *Genesis 4:6-7 (NIV 1984)*

The Lord here is saying to Cain that if he obeys, he will be accepted (protected), but if he chooses to disobey, then sin is crouching at the door, desiring to have him, but he should master it. He will master it through obedience to God. Obedience to God and His Word keeps you protected and shielded from the enemy. Conversely, disobedience opens a door for him to enter. You can see this principle working throughout the Bible. When the Israelites turned away from the Word of the Lord, their enemies had victory over them. When they walked in obedience and godliness, they were blessed and protected by the Lord. We must learn to walk in obedience in all that we do. Many

Christians suffer and go through injuries and wounds because of their own disobedience and rebellion.

You can correct this today by simply repenting, and making a decision to walk in obedience. Just as disobedience opens a door to the enemy, obedience shuts that door and keeps you protected.

> A person's own folly leads to their ruin, yet their heart rages against the LORD.
> *Proverbs 19:3*

Your love for God is measured and demonstrated by obedience. It is not measured by how loud you sing, or how long you pray, but by obedience to His Word. Your love for God is measured by how much you obey Him. When you walk in obedience then you will find yourself walking in the favour and protection of God. Some Christians today want God's favour and believe that praying for it or confessing it will bring it to them. I am not against prayer or confession, but I believe that favour will rest on those who walk in obedience, staying close to the Lord. It is a by-product of godly living.

Keys to healing

1. Repentance

Repentance simply means a change of mind. The first step to healing is making a decision that you want to be healed, and that you want to let go of your hurt and pain. Strangely, some people who are wounded begin to find their identity and even comfort in their wound. Rehearsing the pain and memories of the past is a way to escape their present realities and so they find it difficult to move on from this place of hurt. They have lived for so long with the pain that it has become a part of them, and they cannot remember life without it. They have learned to escape into their bitter, accusing memories. If this is you, it's time to make a quality decision that you have had enough of the hurt, isolation and pain and it's time to move on.

Do not underestimate the power of a decision. So much of life is dependent on first making a decision. In the Christian life, quality choices will move us on into the next level of our walk with the Lord. Many are waiting for something to change or happen, but they do not realise that the change will come as they make a quality decision. I challenge you to make that decision today for your life. You do not have to wait another week or month; you do not have to carry the hurt and pain any longer. Today could be your day of freedom.

2. Forgiveness

It is likely, if you are wounded, that someone has hurt you, and that you may be holding unforgiveness in your heart towards that person. I define forgiveness in the following way: to cease to feel anger and resentment towards a person who has offended you. In essence it is to pardon or free another from a debt.

It is a decision to let go of your hurt, your rights and the pain, a decision to forgive. This decision will release you, and bring you freedom. Ask the Lord to forgive you for holding on to the wounds of the past, the unforgiveness, anger, accusation or bitterness. Tell Him that you are willing to let it all go, and that you need Him to heal you. Once you have talked with the Lord, you may need to talk to others and put things right or ask for forgiveness. Relationships that have been divided or become embittered will need to be restored. The Holy Spirit will take you on a journey of restoration. You may be led to write some letters, to make phone calls, or even to visit people and put things right. Remember, this may be a vulnerable, exposing time, but it is necessary for healing to complete its work. In situations where the offender is no longer alive, perhaps a conversation and prayer with a trusted friend could prove helpful. Though you may find some of these times painful, you will also experience tremendous release and liberty as you obey the Holy Spirit. The weight and burden you may have carried for years will be lifted from your shoulders. A word of wisdom to those who have suffered abuse – not every relationship can be repaired and reconciled. It would be dangerous to go back into an abusive, dysfunctional relationship, but you can and should still release forgiveness and go through the process of healing.

> For if you forgive other people when they sin against you, your heavenly Father will also forgive you. But if you do not forgive others their sins, your Father will not forgive your sins.
> *Matthew 6:14-15*

Many Christians do not realise that their forgiveness from the Lord is conditional on them forgiving those who have hurt them. God forgives you, because you have forgiven others. This is such an important truth; take time to allow it to sink in.

3. *Choose to walk in love*

> Love is patient, love is kind. It does not envy, it does not boast, it is not proud. It is not rude, it is not self-seeking, it is not easily angered, it keeps no record of wrongs. Love does not delight in evil but rejoices with the truth. It always protects, always trusts, always hopes, always perseveres. Love never fails. But where there are prophecies, they will cease; where there are tongues, they will be stilled; where there is knowledge, it will pass away.
> *1 Corinthians 13:4-8 (NIV 1984)*

This is another powerful key not only to bring healing, but it is also a way to protect yourself from future hurt. This passage tells us that 'love never fails'. Prophecies will cease, tongues will be stilled and knowledge will pass away, but love never fails. As believers, we must choose to walk in love. You may say that this is impossible after what was done to you. You may feel that there is no love in you to give out to others. Read this verse:

> And hope does not disappoint us, because God has poured out his love into our hearts by the Holy Spirit, whom he has given us.
> *Romans 5:5 (NIV 1984)*

If you are a believer, then the love of God has been poured into your heart. You may not feel that it is there, but it is. You may have suppressed it because of what you have suffered. If you ask the Holy Spirit to help you to love again, He will. The more you surrender to his voice in every situation, the stronger this love in you will grow. I remember as an eight-year-old boy being the focus of racist comments in my school. I hated going to school, and I felt anger and hatred towards my tormentors. I began to feign sickness so I could escape school. One day my dad sat down with me and explained how to walk in love. He showed me that I had to forgive these people because they did not really understand what they were doing. From that day, a release came into my life. I went back to school with the ability to love those who tormented me with unkind words. The words no longer hurt or found a place to wound me. Love never fails! That one decision to walk in love has influenced my life ever since.

Let me give you a task that will help you to become stronger in the love walk. Write out the verses from 1 Corinthians 13:4-8 and replace the word 'love' with your name. Then take this and make it your confession and prayer every day for thirty days. You will soon see change come into your heart and actions. Love never fails.

4. Time in His presence

> Repent, then, and turn to God, so that your sins may be wiped out, that times of refreshing may come from the Lord.
> *Acts 3:19*

When you spend time in God's presence, it will refresh, cleanse and heal you. You may not be used to this, but make time just to soak in God's presence. Put some worship music on and become intimate with God. Allow Him to love you, and to heal you. Meditate on the following scriptures:

> Better is one day in your courts than a thousand elsewhere; I would rather be a doorkeeper in the house of my God than dwell in the tents of the wicked. For the LORD God is a sun and shield; the LORD bestows favour and honour; no good thing does he withhold from those whose way of life is blameless.
> *Psalms 84:10-11*

> As the deer pants for streams of water, so my soul pants for you, my God. My soul thirsts for God, for the living God. When can I go and meet with God?
> *Psalms 42:1-2*

> Deep calls to deep in the roar of your waterfalls; all your waves and breakers have swept over me.
> *Psalms 42:7*

Things that could take months of counselling can be healed in a moment when in His presence. There is a valid place for counsel and personal ministry, but do not underestimate the power of being in the presence of the living God and allowing Him to pour in His love and make you whole. You must make a decision to come into His presence. The enemy will do all he can to keep you from that place because he knows that your life will be made whole and his power broken. It is not difficult to come into Jesus' presence because we have free access on account of His work on the cross. You may just come quietly meditating on a scripture and talking to God, and in that quietness His presence washes over you. You may put on some worship music, start to love God, and become intimate with Him. These times will become some of your most precious times; you will find yourself living in the place of His presence daily. The car or the walk to work can become your moment of intimacy with God.

5. *Renewing your mind with the Word; use the sword and shield*

> For though we live in the world, we do not wage war as the world does. The weapons we fight with are not the weapons of the world. On the contrary, they have divine power to demolish strongholds. We demolish arguments and every pretension that sets itself up against the knowledge of God, and we take captive every thought to make it obedient to Christ.
> *2 Corinthians 10:3-5*

Your mind is the place in which the greatest battles will be fought. Strongholds are thought patterns that are contrary to the knowledge of God. It is these thought patterns that the enemy uses to access our lives. The enemy uses our negative thoughts as doorways into our lives. We need to pull down strongholds and wrong thought patterns, and replace them with godly thought patterns.

Even after you have been healed of a wound, you will need to change your old thoughts. This will not happen by itself, because you have thought the old negative way for many months, maybe years. You will need to replace these old ways of thinking with God's Word. There is no shortcut to doing this. You have to feed the Word of God into your heart. Read the Bible, listen to audio sermons and read books. If there is a particular stronghold in your life, find scriptures, sermons and books that will combat it.

> Do not conform any longer to the pattern of this world, but be transformed by the renewing of your mind. Then you will be able to test and approve what God's will is – his good, pleasing and perfect will.
> *Romans 12:2*

> To make her holy, cleansing her by the washing with water through the word.
> *Ephesians 5:26*

Overdose on the Bible, night and day feed it in. You will find that the Word of God will wash your thoughts, emotions and memories. You need the Word to do its work in you. Learn to use the Bible both as a sword to attack the enemy and as a shield to protect yourself. If you feed it into your life, the Holy Spirit will help you to learn how to handle the Word.

6. Ask for help

> Just as a body, though one, has many parts, but all its many parts form one body, so it is with Christ.
> *1 Corinthians 12:12*

God has created you to live life in community, and when walking with others your life becomes stronger and richer.

Other people can offer you a listening ear, strength, prayer and accountability. Only in authentic community can we begin to see more clearly. No matter how gifted or spiritually mature you may be, you need other people in your life to help you to hear God and navigate through life.

This might mean that you go to a trusted Christian leader for help and guidance, or to seek a professional counsellor's help. Or it could simply mean that you go to a trusted family member or friend and open up your heart and ask for wisdom and prayer.

Be honest, share from your heart and don't hold things back. Then be careful to hear and to take the counsel that is offered. Sometimes just simply to be able to talk with someone and have them pray with you is enough, but other times they will advise you and give instruction that you will need to follow through. Decide to go all the way to freedom.

Conclusion

It is time for the wounded in the body of Christ to get back in the fight. Healing is available for you today; it is just a prayer away. It is time to stop rehearsing your wounds and living in self-pity. It is time to be healed. Jesus has provided all you need to be made whole. Do not deny your inheritance as a believer. You can move into healing and wholeness today. You are needed, you are loved and you are a valuable part of this end-time army.

Application

- The application for healing has been outlined in the last few pages. Will you make a quality decision to start the journey to healing? This will be the first step to healing and wholeness. Take a few moments of quiet meditation and speak to the Lord. Make the right choice today.

Training – the process of developing fitness and efficiency

Warrior – a person whose occupation is warfare, experienced or distinguished in fighting

Hunger – craving appetite, the uneasy or painful sensation caused by lack

Chapter 5
Building Strong Your Inner Person – Part 1

Importance of the inner person

> I pray that out of his glorious riches he may strengthen you with power through his Spirit in your inner being.
> *Ephesians 3:16*

The end-time Warriors will be strong on the inside. Your spirit needs to be strong. Who you are is far more important than what you do. What you do is a by-product of who you are. So, focus on making sure you are who you are supposed to be. Many times, we are trying to change the fruit without changing the root. Many have been more concerned about actions and lifestyle, not realising that the fruit is always affected by the root. Your actions and lifestyle flow from the inside out. Jesus taught this in the Gospel of Matthew when He said that you can make the fruit of a tree good or bad by making the tree good or bad (see Matthew 12:33). In this chapter, I want to help you to understand how to build up your inner person to make it strong.

> For physical training is of some value, but godliness
> has value for all things, holding promise for both the
> present life and the life to come.
> *1 Timothy 4:8*

This scripture tells us that physical, natural training is of some value, but godliness holds promise for both this life and the one to come. Many are involved in physical training, walking, running, aerobics, weightlifting or swimming. These things are good but godliness, or spiritual training, is far better, holding higher value. I think that we need physically healthy, fit believers today if we are to live long and do what the Lord has called us to do. However, more importantly, we need men and women who have trained and disciplined the spirit person far more than their natural person. You can look great on the outside, but be weak and crippled on the inside.

Just as people put their bodies through discipline and exercise to build muscle and stamina, you will need to do exactly the same thing for your spirit person. How healthy and fit is your inner person? It will take discipline and hard work. The Bible tells us that if we do this, it not only helps us in this life, but also holds promise for the life to come. I believe the Warriors that are being roused on the earth at this time will be strong on the inside. They will be men and women of godliness and discipline. You see, the anointing[5] will help you in ministry, but you need a strong spirit to live each day. You cannot depend on the anointing for daily living and resisting the enemy. Develop your spirit.

You must develop a hunger

The first step in this journey is to get the hunger for it. You will only do that for which you have an appetite. If you are going to develop your inner person, you must get a hunger, a desire to do so. Ask the Holy Spirit to help you and give you new desires. You may think, 'But I am not disciplined or naturally inclined to build up my inner person.' However, hungers and appetites can be cultivated or grown, or weakened or even killed.

> Whatever is submitted to grows stronger, whatever is resisted grows weaker.
> *Ed Cole*[6]

If you deny yourself a thing, then your appetite for it will eventually die. If you keep feeding yourself something, eventually you will develop a hunger for that thing. A few years ago, I realised how bad sugared drinks were for me. I used to drink a lot of fizzy sugar-filled drinks. Instead, I started to drink sparkling water. The first time I tried it, I spat it out. I hated the taste. After a while of denying myself fizzy drinks and sticking to sparkling

---

[5] Anointing is simply God's divine assistance and power on public ministry.

[6] http://www.edcole.org (accessed 23rd January 2018).

water, I developed a liking for sparkling water. If I have a choice now, I will always go for the water. My taste had been changed. This can happen spiritually when you are changing habits and disciplines.

I am told that a habit can be made or broken in about thirty days. Thirty days of disciplined, forced action can make or break a habit. There is no habit that cannot be changed. I trust that this gives you hope to become the person God created you to be. The Lord wants to help you, and as you look to Him and depend on His strength, it will become much easier.

> Blessed are those who hunger and thirst for righteousness, for they will be filled.
> *Matthew 5:6*

I want to give you some spiritual disciplines that you need to build into your life. You can get a desire for these things so that you enjoy doing them, but it will also be a discipline. Many Christians do not like discipline. They would rather someone preach it into them, or lay hands on them and pray it into them. It does not work like that. You will need to work with God's Word and the Holy Spirit! These are spiritual habits enabled by God's grace, so they could be also be called 'habits of grace'.

The discipline of God's Word

The Word of God must be alive in you. The Bible is your source of food and spiritual nourishment. Without regular intake of the Bible, you will be weak. It is important that you feed the Word of God into yourself. It is not enough just to hear a sermon once a week. Just as you need to eat every day, so you need the food of the Word every day to feed your spirit and keep it healthy.

> If we would know God and be godly we must know the Word of God intimately.
> *Donald S Whitney*[7]

The Bible tells us:

> Do not let this Book of the Law depart from your mouth; meditate on it day and night, so that you may be careful to do everything written in it. Then you will be prosperous and successful.
> *Joshua 1:8 (NIV 1984)*

The Warriors I am talking about will be firmly grounded upon the Word of God. They will love the Word, know the Word and live the Word. The Word will live in them as they live out the Word of God every day. They will know that their strength and energy comes from the Word. It is the Word that will stop them going into error. Here are five ways to take the Word into your life. If you want to be strong and balanced you will need to build these things into your life as regular disciplines:

- Hearing the Word;
- Reading the Word;

---

[7] Donald S Whitney, *Spiritual Disciplines for the Christian Life* (Colorado Springs, CO: NavPress, 2006).

- Studying the Word;

- Memorising the Word;

- Meditating on the Word.

1. Hearing

> Faith comes by hearing, and hearing by the word of
> God.
> *Romans 10:17 (NKJV)*

> Devote yourself to the public reading of Scripture.
> *1 Timothy 4:13*

This is probably the easiest way to take in the Bible, but it will still require a certain amount of discipline and commitment. If Paul is telling Timothy to be devoted to reading the Word publicly, there must have been others who were devoted to hearing the Word being proclaimed. I believe that we need to hear the Word of God preached. When I was young I invested in a portable cassette tape player and spent many hours listening to teaching tapes. Today it is so easy to listen to godly podcasts and sermons from all over the world. There is a place for that and it is a real blessing. But there is still a place for belonging to a church family and listening each week live to the Bible being preached. It has the power to change and make us into who God has called us to be. Do not use excuses to stay away from the house of God. Audio messages and Christian programmes can be a great encouragement, but they are not a substitute for going to church and listening to the Bible being opened up to you. If you want great faith, it will come by hearing the Word. You need to put the Word of God into your heart.

2. *Reading*

> All Scripture is God-breathed and is useful for teaching, rebuking, correcting and training in righteousness, so that the servant of God may be thoroughly equipped for every good work.
> *2 Timothy 3:16-17*

The Scriptures are vital for our godliness and growth. Therefore, we need to make it a daily habit to read the Word. It is not enough just to hear a sermon once or twice a week. That is good, but it is not enough. You need the Word daily. You may not be a great reader, but the Lord will grant you grace to read. I have met people who were not confident readers, but regularly reading the Bible has improved their confidence and ability. Read systematically, and have a plan that you are following. Do not just open up in a different place every day. There are many good plans available online;[8] follow one of them so you can work your way through the whole of Scripture. Have a regular time and place each day when you read. This will make it easier to develop a lifestyle habit.

---

[8] For example, https://www.ligonier.org/blog/bible-reading-plans/ (accessed 24th January 2018).

3. Studying

> Study to shew thyself approved unto God, a workman that needeth not to be ashamed, rightly dividing the word of truth.
> *2 Timothy 2:15 (KJV)*

Reading will give you an overview, but studying God's Word will give you a greater depth and confidence. You may not have time to study the Bible each day, so set apart a time each week. You do not have to be clever or academic to study the Bible. In Acts 17, the Bereans were called noble because they heard the Word, and then went away to examine it for themselves. We need people like this in the Church today. Yes, listen to the sermons your pastor preaches, but also examine the Bible for yourself. Then you will mature. You may choose to study a particular Bible book, a character, a topic such as faith or prayer, or you may do a part-time course with an online Bible school. The Holy Spirit will be your teacher, the one who brings fresh insights and revelations to you. Set a regular time each week when you will do this, and have a plan of what you are doing.

4. Memorising

King David said:

> I have hidden your word in my heart
> that I might not sin against you.
> Praise be to you, LORD;
> teach me your decrees.
> With my lips I recount

all the laws that come from your mouth.
I rejoice in following your statutes
as one rejoices in great riches.
I meditate on your precepts
and consider your ways.
I delight in your decrees;
I will not neglect your word.
Psalm 119:11-16

He had learned the secret power of hiding God's Word in his heart. Read what Chuck Swindoll says about memorising scripture:

I know of no other single practice in the Christian life more rewarding, practically speaking, than learning scripture. That's right. No other single exercise pays greater spiritual dividends. Your prayer life will be sharpened; your witness will be sharper and more effective. Your counselling will be in demand. Your attitudes and outlook will begin to change. Your mind will become more alert and observant. Your confidence and assurance will be enhanced. Your faith will be solidified.
Chuck Swindoll[9]

Wow, all that from memorising the Word of God. For many today, this is a forgotten discipline. You must regain it in order to fulfil all the Lord has for you. If your Bible were taken away from you, then what you have hidden in

---

[9] Cited in Whitney, *Spiritual Disciplines*.

your heart will sustain you. The Word will keep you from sin, and sharpen your thinking and daily life. Read that quotation again. Some may say that they are no good at remembering Scripture, and yet they will remember songs or jokes and other trivia. You can remember. The Holy Spirit will help you. Learn to remember things word for word. Write down the verse on a piece of card and the reference on the other side. Carry these cards around with you and make use of them throughout the day, or you may save them as I now do as screen shots on my phone. First thing in the morning and last thing at night, go through your cards. Use times when you are travelling or waiting in queues to memorise. This one discipline can revolutionise your life.

5. Meditating

> Finally, brothers and sisters, whatever is true, whatever is noble, whatever is right, whatever is pure, whatever is lovely, whatever is admirable – if anything is excellent or praiseworthy – think about such things.
> *Philippians 4:8*

This really goes hand in hand with memorising. One will help the other. When you meditate on the Word, it will wash and cleanse you. In Ephesians 5:26 the apostle Paul talks about the water of God's Word, cleansing. Learn to take a verse or passage and think upon it, allowing it to cleanse you, and ask the Holy Spirit for fresh revelation from it. These scriptures will become your thoughts during the day, and will help you stay focused and in tune with your master – Jesus. Many believers today are thinking and rehearsing the wrong things in their minds. Your thoughts are seeds and they will produce a harvest for you. A person with negative thoughts will produce negative actions and lifestyle. You need to make sure the Word has a prominent place in your thought life. This will cause the fruit of the Word to be seen in your life.

Application

We have looked at three things in this chapter. The importance of the inner person, developing hunger and the high value of the Word of God. Clear instruction has been given to help you apply these things to your life.

* Will you take a few moments to reflect, and think upon what you need to do?

* It is time to make some quality decisions to start building strong your inner person by feeding on the Word.

* Pray and commit these things to the Lord.

Pray – ask earnestly or humbly, beseech, make devout supplication to God, commune, commune with God

Holy – sanctified, separated to God, wholly His

Strong – able to withstand force, pressure or wear

Chapter 6
Building Strong Your Inner Person – Part 2

The discipline of prayer

> If you have the Spirit without the Word, you blow up. If you have the Word without the Spirit, you dry up. If you have both the Word and the Spirit, you grow up.
>
> *Anonymous*

You may have heard this saying before, but it is true. You need both the Word and the Spirit (prayer) to have a balanced mature life.

Prayer is simply communion with God. Communication is needed to keep any relationship healthy. If the communication is not good, frequent, honest and open, then the relationship will not grow into greater intimacy. On the other hand, good communication will develop a healthy relationship. By prayer, I mean talking to God, praising God and worshipping God. There are also different types of prayer – thanksgiving, petition, intercession etc. It is not my desire to go into all of these in this book. However, I simply want to stress that prayer is an essential tool for building strong your inner person. This end-time army will be praying Warriors.

Jesus, our example

> Very early in the morning, while it was still dark, Jesus got up, left the house and went off to a solitary place, where he prayed.
> *Mark 1:35*

> Jesus often withdrew to lonely places and prayed.
> *Luke 5:16*

First, Jesus is our example in that He prayed. If there were anyone that walked the earth who did not need to pray, it would be Jesus. Yet we see that He prayed. He had a regular habit of withdrawing to pray. It was a discipline in His life. He is our best example. If He needed to pray, you and I need to pray. So many believers do not pray, or do not pray enough. I am not trying to get people to pray because of religious duty or legalism. Prayer is essential to keep our communion alive with God, and it is God's ordained way of bringing change to our world. If you are a believer and you do not pray, you need to repent today and ask God to give you a hunger to pray, and to teach you to pray.

> And when you pray …
> *Matthew 6:5*

But when you pray …
Matthew 6:6

And when you pray …
Matthew 6:7

This, then, is how you should pray …
Matthew 6:9

So I say to you: ask and it will be given to you; seek and you will find; knock and the door will be opened to you.
Luke 11:9

Second, Jesus taught us to pray. These things were not taught as an option to those who may want to pray, but as a requirement. It is essential for every believer to be praying. A very simple and basic truth is that the more we pray, the more answers to prayer we will experience. We are commanded by Jesus to ask, to seek and to knock. Every Christian should be praying daily. Relationship with our Saviour is our lifeline, and prayer is the way we keep that relationship alive. The reason many believers are spiritually dry and their hearts cold is that they have neglected this vital command.

As it is the business of tailors to make clothes, and of cobblers to mend shoes, so it is the business of Christians to pray.
Martin Luther[10]

---

[10] Gary L Thomas, *Simply Sacred* (Grand Rapids, MI: Zondervan, 2011).

You can learn how to pray

In Luke 11, Jesus' disciples asked Him to teach them to pray. It is not only possible to learn how to pray, but also essential if we are to grow. In our marriages, we learn over time how to communicate better with our partners, and how to interpret more easily what they are saying. So we must grow in our prayer life and intimacy with the Lord.

First, you can learn how to pray by praying. This is the most effective way of learning. The most effective way to learn a musical instrument is by playing it. We learn a new language by speaking it. Yes, mistakes may be made, but it is a sure way to grow in your praying. I encourage you to have a regular time in a day set aside for prayer. It does not have to be a very long time to start with, but you do need to make time.

Pray with others who are further on than you are. Their company will sharpen you. It says in Proverbs 27:17: 'As iron sharpens iron, so one person sharpens another.' You will find yourself learning as you pray with others; it will stretch you and grow you. We are a body, and one part of the body helps the others to grow. Value these relationships and make time to pray with others.

Second, you can learn how to pray by reading about prayer. There are many good books on prayer. Read books that will teach you how to pray; and read the life stories of those who were powerful in prayer. Some authors you could read are George Müller, Andrew Murray and E M Bounds. These books will inspire you and help you. I encourage you to read.

God answers prayer

> Ask and it will be given to you; seek and you will find; knock and the door will be opened to you. For everyone who asks receives; the one who seeks finds; and to the one who knocks, the door will be opened.
>
> *Matthew 7:7-8*

We are not praying for the sake of praying, but because we believe God answers prayer. Mountains move, situations change and miracles happen when believers pray. Read your Bible, and see that when people turned to God in prayer, things changed. Look at history, and see the same things. We need people today who know how to get business done in prayer. This will happen when we realise the power in prayer, and that it does change situations. We have many who will complain about situations, but not many who will pray and see the situation turned. Warriors of prayer are needed today.

Two ways to pray

Many different things could be taught on prayer. There are many styles and ways to pray. There are times to intercede. There are times to love the Lord in gentle worship and whispered conversation, there are times of high praise and thanksgiving. There are times of impassioned petition with tears before God's throne and there are times of adoring silence. Every Warrior must be a worshipper; our ability to war is in direct correlation to our intimacy in worship.

Develop a sweet intimacy with Jesus in your prayer and worship.

I want to emphasise two things that I believe are key for these end-time Warriors. First, strong, declaring, faith-filled prayers; and second, praying in the Holy Spirit (tongues).

1. Strong, declaring prayers

> 'Now, Lord, consider their threats and enable your servants to speak your word with great boldness. Stretch out your hand to heal and perform signs and wonders through the name of your holy servant Jesus.' After they prayed, the place where they were meeting was shaken. And they were all filled with the Holy Spirit and spoke the word of God boldly.
> *Acts 4:29-31*

We need to pray strong, declaring prayers that are filled with faith. Too many are weak and apologetic in the way they pray. I do not just mean loudness. Strength is not about volume, but about the inner confidence in the one to whom you are praying, and your privileged position as a believer. Much of the New Testament prayer is a declaration and strong confession. In the passage above, we read a prayer of the early disciples. They had just been warned not to speak in the name of Jesus, and then released. They went immediately to prayer, but their prayers were not motivated by fear, insecurity or self-preservation. They prayed boldly for more of God's power, and greater boldness to speak the truth. There was a strong sense of faith in the way that they prayed. They expected

God to hear their prayer, and to answer their request. They knew that the Great Commission had been left to them, and that they needed power and boldness to carry out the task. You too need to learn to pray strong in faith and with confidence as the Early Church did. Walk in your God-given authority as a believer who is on a mission for their master.

> From the days of John the Baptist until now, the kingdom of heaven has been forcefully advancing, and forceful men lay hold of it.
> *Matthew 11:12 (NIV 1984)*

Jesus is helping us to understand that there is a clash of two kingdoms and that the advance of His kingdom is done with intentional force. He is clear that the kingdom of God is 'forcefully advancing', and that you need to be forceful to advance it. Prayer is an important factor in advancing God's kingdom and purposes on the earth. In fact, nothing happens unless people are first praying.

We have had a certain level of praying and that has been good, but we need to develop strong, declaring prayers. God is raising men and women of holy violence who will know how to get results in the spirit realm. Praying this strongly may even offend your mind to start with, but listen to your spirit and develop a strong prayer life.

The most powerful prayers are those that come into agreement with what God is saying, and pray back to Him what He reveals to us: 'Your kingdom come, your will be done' (Matthew 6:10). So praying the Bible is a very legitimate way to pray. There are many psalms that can be prayed and also many apostolic prayers[11] too. These are the prayers we read in the epistles written by the apostles. Praying God's Word back to Him is powerful, life-giving and biblical, and we can do so with confidence.

2. *Praying in tongues*

> I thank God that I speak in tongues more than all of you.
> *1 Corinthians 14:18*

> And pray in the Spirit on all occasions with all kinds of prayers and requests. With this in mind, be alert and always keep on praying for all the Lord's people.
> *Ephesians 6:18*

Some Christians pray in tongues, others do not. If you are a believer in Jesus, then this gift of praying in the Spirit is for you. It is not just for a few or a special elect. On a trip to India a number of years ago, I spoke about the baptism of the Holy Spirit to a room full of children aged four to eleven years. After about twenty-five minutes of teaching, we laid hands on these young children, they were baptised with the Holy Spirit, and began to speak in other tongues; we witnessed many of them having encounters with God, experiencing His love. God is no respecter of persons, culture or age. All you have to do is ask Him, and believe that you will receive. Either you can ask another believer to pray for you to receive the Holy Spirit, or you can go

---

[11] http://www.mikebickle.org.edgesuite.net/MikeBickleVOD/2014/Apostolic_Prayers.9_pages.pdf (accessed 24th January 2018).

directly to the Lord in worship and ask Him to baptise you with the Holy Spirit.

Many of those who do speak in tongues do not use this gift to its fullest potential. Some only speak in quiet murmuring tongues, almost embarrassed to speak out. Many do not regularly pray in the Spirit. This gift was not given for you to look or act religious. It was given because God has ordained praying in the Spirit as a means of receiving more grace personally and for the world around us.

> But you, dear friends, *build yourselves up* in your
> most holy faith and *pray in the Holy Spirit.*
> *Jude 1:20 (NIV 1984, my emphases)*

Praying in the Spirit will make your inner person strong. The apostle Paul said that he spoke in tongues more than all the Corinthian church (see 1 Corinthians 14:18)! There will be occasions when you will not know how to pray, and then you will need to pray in the Spirit.

The tongues that you have will develop with use. They will become stronger and more articulate. You will also be given more words to speak. Many are still only speaking the few words that they received when they were baptised in the Spirit. You need to move on from there, and the only way to do this is to grow by using and exercising the gift. When my children were younger they developed their use of the English language and have grown in understanding as they have grown in age. They now have greater freedom with words and do not get frustrated at not being able to communicate. You must develop your gift of speaking in tongues in the same way. Do not leave it at the same level, stretch for more.

You need to make a daily time when you will pray in tongues. You need to pray with strength, loud enough for your ears to hear you. Do not be apologetic or embarrassed about praying in the Spirit. When I first started out in ministry as a teenager, I began a ministry called Christian Warriors that was involved in youth and schools work. We used to travel around the country taking meetings and doing evangelism. Without fail, we would pray for about an hour before each meeting or event. We would worship, pray strong in English and pray in tongues. Those times of prayer would often change the atmosphere of the place in which we were about to minister. It would also cause faith and expectancy to rise in our own spirits. We felt stronger after praying, and prepared to minister. For me that was one of our key strategies to successful meetings.

When you first start to do these things, your flesh will not like it, and will have to be disciplined. Your mind will tell you to stop, and you will wonder what you are doing. Very quickly, these thoughts will go, and after a few days or a week, you will feel the strength in your own spirit from praying in tongues. The flesh and mind are often offended by the spirit. That is why we must learn to obey the Word by faith, not by feelings.

This may be new to you, or it may simply serve as a reminder. Either way you will benefit greatly if you start praying strong this way. You cannot survive these end days with wimpy, apologetic prayers that have no faith connected to them.

The discipline of holiness

Holiness is simply separation to God. Just as I am holy to my wife because I love her and am devoted to her, I am holy to the Lord and devoted to Him. It means you belong to the Lord, and you live your life to please Him. Holiness is not about rules, regulations or a certain dress code, it is about our hearts being captivated by Jesus.

It is commanded

> Therefore, I urge you, brothers and sisters, in view of God's mercy, to offer your bodies as a living sacrifice, holy and pleasing to God – this is your true and proper worship.
> *Romans 12:1*

> As obedient children, do not conform to the evil desires you had when you lived in ignorance. But just as he who called you is holy, so be holy in all you do; for it is written: 'Be holy, because I am holy.' Since you call on a Father who judges each person's work impartially, live out your time as foreigners here in reverent fear.
> *1 Peter 1:14-17*

Holiness is not an option for the believer, it is commanded. We need to be holy just as He is holy (see Leviticus 19:2). Paul urges us to offer our bodies as living sacrifices. Sacrifices do not have a say in what happens to them; they are dead to themselves. This biblical teaching isn't very popular in the Church today, but it is essential if we desire to become strong and see the power of God transform us and the world around us. There can be no mixture. We also must die to our own fleshly nature, and allow the life of Christ to become stronger and more evident in us.

> Since we have these promises, dear friends, let us purify ourselves from everything that contaminates body and spirit, perfecting holiness out of reverence for God.
> *2 Corinthians 7:1*

I believe that we should be growing in our holiness daily. So many believers have settled at a particular level. Instead of using the Bible as their standard, they use other Christians, or worse, they use the world in which we live. Our world is becoming more evil and corrupt, and is pushing the limit of what is acceptable. Sadly, many in the Church have been infected by the world. We need to purify ourselves from all that would contaminate our bodies and spirits.

The power connection

> Make every effort to live in peace with everyone and to be holy; without holiness no one will see the Lord.
> *Hebrews 12:14*

I believe that holiness is the power connection. It will allow the Holy Spirit's power to flow through you unhindered. I know that the least believer in the kingdom has the right to use the name of Jesus, and to pray for the sick expecting them to be healed. I believe that is right and correct. But I also believe that the more you give of your heart to Jesus, and the stronger that He lives in you, the greater will be the flow of power from your life. This is not about works or impressing Jesus, but about being broken and dying to self, and allowing Him to live through you. I believe both the Bible and history confirm this. If you want to see more of the Lord in your life, give more of your life to the Lord!

Holiness in thought

> Finally, brothers and sisters, whatever is true, whatever is noble, whatever is right, whatever is pure, whatever is lovely, whatever is admirable – if anything is excellent or praiseworthy – think about such things.
> *Philippians 4:8*

Our thoughts must be pure and holy. Some may think that, because their thoughts are private and no one sees them, they are OK to think anything they like. The Bible teaches us to be holy and pure in our thought life. As I have said before, your thoughts are seeds, and if you allow thoughts to settle into your heart, they will eventually germinate and become trees bearing fruit. You must be careful to pull all thoughts into line with the Word of God. The greatest battles are fought in the mind. Strongholds are built in the mind and the enemy uses the strongholds – wrong thought patterns – as access points into your life (see 2 Corinthians 10:3-5). Be holy in your thoughts.

All sin starts as a thought. Therefore, if we can learn to be holy in our thinking it will help us to be holy with our words and actions. Please do not underestimate the power

of your thoughts. Bring them into obedience with the Word
of God.

Holiness in word

> The tongue has the power of life and death, and
> those who love it will eat its fruit.
> *Proverbs 18:21*

> For, 'Whoever would love life and see good days
> must keep their tongue from evil and their lips from
> deceitful speech.'
> *1 Peter 3:10*

The Bible says that the 'tongue has the power of life and
death'. Your words can build up, or tear down. They can
bring glory to God, or shame to your Christian witness. So
many are careless in how they handle their words, not
realising that there is tremendous power in their speech.
With the same mouth, they can sing praises to God on
Sunday, and then on Monday they can curse someone. This
is not right; we need to choose to be holy in our speech. The
apostle Paul says, 'Let your conversation be always full of
grace, seasoned with salt, so that you may know how to
answer everyone' (Colossians 4:6).

Make this scripture your prayer. Ask God to help you to
be full of grace, seasoned with salt in the way you speak to
others. You may think that this is impossible for you, but I
want to encourage you that this is not beyond your reach.
Ask God for His help; He will help you to change. Do not
think that your present behaviour is acceptable, and that
you are doomed to be this way all your life. You can

change. The world should be able to tell that there is something different about you because of your godly speech.

Holiness in deed (action)

> Live such good lives among the pagans that, though they accuse you of doing wrong, they may see your good deeds and glorify God on the day he visits us.
> *1 Peter 2:12*

> And we pray this in order that you may live a life worthy of the Lord and may please him in every way: bearing fruit in every good work, growing in the knowledge of God.
> *Colossians 1:10 (NIV 1984)*

Our lives as believers need to be an example to others around us. There seems so little difference today between believers and unbelievers. This is wrong; there should be a strong contrast between believers and unbelievers. Our lives should be lived in holiness according to God's purposes as a believer in Jesus. Learn to ask yourself in every setting, 'What would Jesus do in this situation?' Then act accordingly. We belong to a kingdom that has a unique set of values and particular view of all things. These values and God's perspective should shape the way we live each day. People are watching your life and actions. You may not be aware of it, but they are. You are an ambassador of Jesus. You represent Him on this earth; let your life shine out His goodness and grace. The early disciples were called Christians, which simply means 'little Christ'. They acted and behaved so much like Jesus that people called them Christians. Are you a Christian?

How to be holy – it is a decision

> But Daniel *purposed* in his heart that he would not defile himself with the portion of the king's delicacies, nor with the wine which he drank; therefore he requested of the chief of the eunuchs that he might not defile himself.
> *Daniel 1:8 (NKJV, my emphasis)*

Quite simply, you have to choose to be holy. You cannot have someone pray for you and make you holy; or preach to you and make you holy. You choose to be holy, choose to say no to some things and yes to others. Warriors need to make strong choices, not just have wishful thinking. Many people wish to be or to do something. Go beyond that to a quality decision that you make. Daniel purposed in his heart not to defile himself. You too must purpose in your heart not to defile yourself.

The Bible

> How can a young person stay on the path of purity? By living according to your word. I seek you with all my heart; do not let me stray from your commands. I have hidden your word in my heart that I might not sin against you.
> *Psalm 119:9-11*

> To make her holy, cleansing her by the washing with
> water through the word.
> *Ephesians 5:26*

The Word of God is a powerful weapon that you have been given that will help you to resist the enemy. As I have said earlier, it also has the ability to wash you clean as you read it. Owning a Bible or having it on your phone is not enough. You must feed it into your heart for it to be of help to you. If the Word is in your heart, you will find the Holy Spirit drawing it out of your spirit when you need it. Many years ago, someone said to me, 'This book will keep you from sin, or sin will keep you from this book.' How true I have found that to be.

The Bible will help you by washing you while you read it. We live in a dirty world, and sometimes we pick up stuff in our daily lives, attitudes, thoughts or emotions. Nevertheless, when you read the Word it will wash all those things away, and correct attitudes, thoughts and emotions in your life. I have literally felt the Word washing me inside as I have read it. I have felt the pressures and conversations of the day washed from me. I have been left feeling clean and energised.

Follow the Holy Spirit

> Those who live according to the sinful nature have
> their minds set on what that nature desires; but those
> who live in accordance with the Spirit have their
> minds set on what the Spirit desires. The mind of
> sinful man is death, but the mind controlled by the
> Spirit is life and peace.
> *Romans 8:5-6 (NIV 1984)*

If you are a believer, then the Holy Spirit lives inside you, and you must learn to listen to and obey the Holy Spirit. Learn to tune in your spiritual ears by asking the Holy Spirit what you should do. The more you listen to Him, the stronger His leading and voice will become. This a most exciting and adventurous way to live. If this is new to you, simply pray and ask the Holy Spirit to help you live today as He would want you to do. You have a choice, whether to live by the sinful nature, or empowered by the Holy Spirit. Choose today to follow the Spirit.

Fall in love with Jesus

> Jesus replied: 'Love the Lord your God with all your heart and with all your soul and with all your mind.'
> *Matthew 22:37*

> I know your deeds, your hard work and your perseverance. I know that you cannot tolerate wicked people, that you have tested those who claim to be apostles but are not, and have found them false. You have persevered and have endured hardships for my name, and have not grown weary. Yet I hold this against you: you have forsaken the love you had at first.
> *Revelation 2:2-4*

This is the most effective way to be holy. If you fall in love with Jesus, you will want to please Him in your thoughts, words and actions. It will also keep you away from the trap of becoming legalistic, and having a list of dos and don'ts. If your love for Jesus has grown cold then you need to repent – change your mind about your state. Ask Him to help you to rebuild your relationship with Him. Start talking to him every day. Spend time in worship, adore Him and allow Him to have the rightful place in your heart again. It is easy to live holy when you are in love with Him.

A few times in the early years of my married life, I found myself becoming too busy, and neglecting the relationship with my wife. We began to feel coldness and indifference creeping in. I had to make time in my schedule, so that both of us could be alone and together. Then I had to speak honestly with her, and ask for her forgiveness. We spent time in conversation together, and the relationship was restored. You may need to do this very thing with the Lord. Fall in love again, as you realise just how much He loves you. He is waiting for you today!

Application

We have looked at two disciplines in this chapter, prayer and holiness. As well as emphasising their importance, these things require a decision and then a commitment.

- What do you need to do to make these disciplines a part of your daily life?

- Will you make the decision to do that?

- Ask God for grace and to enable you to do all that the Bible requires of you.

Characteristic – defining feature: a feature or quality that makes somebody or something recognisable

Militant – aggressive, extremely active in the defence or support of a cause, often in ways that other people find unacceptable

Bold – fearless and daring, clear and distinct, somewhat overstepping usual bounds or conventional rules, standing up for something

Chapter 7
Characteristics of the End-Time Army – Part 1

The army that is being raised by the Holy Spirit in these days will have certain characteristics that are a very strong part of their lives. These characteristics will be seen in each of the Warriors that make up the army. The characteristics will not come by hoping or wishing for them. They will need to be developed and cultivated in the Warrior's life. It is something you choose to build into your life.

> Have nothing to do with godless myths and old wives' tales; rather, train yourself to be godly. For physical training is of some value, but godliness has value for all things, holding promise for both the present life and the life to come.
> *1 Timothy 4:7-8*

Remember, just as a natural soldier needs to be trained and developed, you too will need to take these things and apply them to your life. You will need to train yourself in these characteristics to make them a strong part of your life. To do this will require a quality decision and then discipline. In this chapter, I want to go through four of these characteristics.

1. Focus

The dictionary defines focus as:

> **Main emphasis:** concentrated effort or attention on a particular thing
> **Seeing sharply:** the condition of seeing sharply and clearly

> And it came to pass, when the time was come that he should be received up, he stedfastly set his face to go to Jerusalem,
> And sent messengers before his face: and they went, and entered into a village of the Samaritans, to make ready for him. And they did not receive him, because his face was as though he would go to Jerusalem.
> *Luke 9:51-53 (KJV)*

In this passage, it talks about Jesus' face being set towards Jerusalem. The people who saw Him could tell that He was focused on going to Jerusalem. Jesus knew what He was called to do, and that He only had a set amount of time on the earth. He did not waste His time, but focused on fulfilling the task that His Father had set Him. He lived thirty-three and a half years, only three and a half of them spent in ministry. He did not allow Himself to waste time, or to be involved with civilian affairs.

> No one serving as a soldier gets entangled in civilian affairs, but rather tries to please his commanding officer.
> *2 Timothy 2:4*

He said in John 5 that He only did what He saw His Father doing. He was focused on obeying the commission given to Him by His Father. Each day He desired to do only what the Father had ordained for Him to do. He was focused. Many Christians today are involved in too many things and have become distracted from their God-given calling.

One of the most effective strategies of the enemy is to distract believers. Sometimes we are focused on good things, or even God things, but they are still distractions from our calling. Very subtly, the enemy has many people majoring on minors, and spending time and energy on things that are not that important. They have become distracted from the real call on their lives. This can happen to an individual, a family or even a church. Many churches are no longer doing the work that Jesus left for them to do, but have been distracted.

I once went out to a restaurant with Esther, my wife. We were looking forward to some good food, and to enjoy each other's company. First, we were made to wait because the tables were not ready, even though we were the only customers in the restaurant. Then, after about ten minutes, we were taken to a table by a waiter. We had just sat down when a waitress came to us and asked us why we were sitting at this table. I explained that another waiter had just seated us. She then made us move to another table. After a long while, menus were brought out and the order taken. We waited, and waited and waited, but there was no sign of food. There were plenty of staff around, some standing, some cleaning glasses which were on empty tables. I asked one of the waiters if our food was ready and, following a further wait, it eventually arrived. I was a little upset as we left that restaurant and have never been back there again. The restaurant is there to serve good food to the customer. However, they ignored us. They seemed to be more interested in the restaurant than in the clientele. What is the use of having a great-looking restaurant with sparkling glasses, if the customers are mistreated and forgotten? They were distracted and had lost their focus, which should have been to serve good food to the customer, and make their experience a pleasant and enjoyable one.

As I was reflecting on this later that afternoon, the Holy Spirit spoke to me, and said that this was the same problem with the Church. We are here for those who do not yet know Jesus, but we have lost our focus. We have nice buildings and we want to make them sparkle. We have great programmes and activities, but we have forgotten the people. It is all about the people, especially those who do not yet come to our churches but live in our communities.

It is time to be focused again, and to remember our calling. The end-time Warriors that God is raising will have the ability to live their lives focused on what God has called them to do. Learn to deal with distractions in a godly way. The apostle Paul is a good example of a focused Warrior.

> I only know that in every city the Holy Spirit warns
> me that prison and hardships are facing me.
> However, I consider my life worth nothing to me, if
> only I may finish the race and complete the task the
> Lord Jesus has given me – the task of testifying to the
> gospel of God's grace.
> *Acts 20:23-24 (NIV 1984)*

Paul could have become distracted and lost his focus because of hardship, prison and a bad environment. His response is a challenge to us: 'I consider my life worth nothing to me, if only I may finish the race and complete the task the Lord Jesus has given me'. He is saying that it does not matter what you do to me, my concern is to do what the Lord has given me to do. I will not be distracted, but will remain focused on the task given to me.

When I was a teenager, I was invited to take a team abroad for ministry. This would be our first overseas missions trip. A great opportunity but, looking back, I wasted it because I became distracted. I was distracted because the weather was too hot, there were too many flies and mosquitoes and I was homesick. I lost my focus and purpose, and I missed a God-given opportunity. I still wonder what would have happened had I handled my task and myself with greater diligence and focus. It is too late for that now, but I have learned from that mistake, and have been careful to handle God opportunities wisely since. I have had to teach myself to stay focused when distraction comes my way.

How to stay focused

- Remind yourself daily of what your purpose on the earth is. Learn to speak this out, and make it something you confess each morning.

- Ask the Holy Spirit for grace to stay focused. I believe that God will grant grace and His empowering to those who ask for it. For years, I underestimated the power of God's grace, and tried much in my own strength.

- Evaluate your life regularly, at the end of a day, week, month and year. This simple exercise will help you to look at your life, learn from the past, and then change whatever needs to be changed. Then you can plan the coming season of life better.

2. Boldness

The dictionary defines a bold person as:

> **Fearless and adventurous:** willing to face adventure and danger with a sense of confidence and fearlessness
> Somewhat overstepping usual bounds, or conventional rules

This army will be fearless and their lives will be lived out as an adventure. They will not bow to conventional rules, or conform to the culture around them; instead, they will be loyal to kingdom culture above any other. They will have a boldness that comes from an unshakeable confidence in God and His Word. They believe what He has spoken more than their circumstances or the lies of the enemy.

> The wicked flee though no one pursues, but the righteous are as bold as a lion.
> *Proverbs 28:1*

The wicked will flee, not the righteous. You are righteous because of the blood of Jesus that cleanses you (see Romans 5:19; 2 Corinthians 5:21). We have been timid and shy for too long. Some Christians live their lives in an embarrassed, apologetic way because of the fear of man. It is time to stop apologising for being a Christian, and to stand up strong and bold. I am always humbled and inspired by the stories of the persecuted Church around the world who are living unashamedly under the threat of persecution and even death. I had Brother Yun (The Heavenly Man), [12] a Chinese Church leader, come and spend a few days at our church to minister for me. He had spent years in prison for his faith in Christ and yet never denied the Lord but kept a firm witness and love for Jesus.

The Bible does not say that you will be bold, but that you will be 'as bold as a lion'. Lions are called 'the kings of the jungle'. They are fearless, confident, and walk in that manner. Their roar can be heard throughout the whole jungle. So many believers have been more like a house cat than a lion. When my daughters were younger they were afraid of cats, but they learned that if they stamped their

---

[12] See Brother Yun, *The Heavenly Man: The Remarkable True Story of Chinese Christian Brother Yun* (Oxford: Monarch, 2002).

feet hard enough the cat would run away. They would have had the shock of their lives if the cat had run towards them instead of running from them. It is time to stop running from the enemy when he stamps his feet. Shock him, turn around and in boldness live out your faith in Jesus!

> Fear of man will prove to be a snare, but whoever trusts in the LORD is kept safe.
> *Proverbs 29:25*

Fear of man is a snare, a trap. If you live with this fear, it will ensnare you, limit you, box you in, and confine your potential. I remember when I first took on the All Nations Church and became the pastor. I was preaching in the first evening service. I looked out at the people, and they were intimidating. Some of them thought I was too young to be the pastor, others did not like me, and I felt intimidated standing there preaching. I could feel my words were dry, with no anointing and no flow. I wanted the meeting to be over, and to be out of the church. The fear of man had trapped me, and therefore there was no liberty in that meeting. I quickly concluded the message and went back to my seat as the worship team led in a closing song. Then the Holy Spirit spoke to me from the above verse in Proverbs, and gave the revelation of what was happening. The spirit of intimidation had trapped me, and stopped me flowing in my gift. I was more concerned about what people thought of me than speaking God's word to those He loves.

As I realised what had happened, I went to the pulpit again and spoke to the people. I read the verse from

Proverbs, and explained that I had preached with a strong sense of the fear of man on me. I told them that it would not happen again, that I would break the fear of man over my life, and that I would only have a righteous, holy fear of God. To my surprise, they responded with applause and loud Amens! Fear will cause you to lose perspective, and things will be blown out of proportion. They will seem bigger than they really are. You must break this spirit of fear by hitting it with boldness.

> For this reason I remind you to fan into flame the gift of God, which is in you through the laying on of my hands. For God did not give us a spirit of timidity, but a spirit of power, of love and of self-discipline.
> *2 Timothy 1:6-7 (NIV 1984)*

Paul had to remind Timothy to stop being intimidated, and to stir up the gift of God that was in him. Who had to do the stirring up? Timothy! You must learn to stir the gift of God in you. God has not given you a spirit of fear or intimidation, but one of power, love and self-discipline. You break the power of the enemy by hitting it with the opposite spirit. So if you feel intimidated, allow boldness to hit the atmosphere. If you are in a situation of hate and anger, then release love.

These end-time Warriors will be as bold as lions. They will follow their master, who is called 'The Lion of the tribe of Judah'. Together they will advance the kingdom of God across nations.

How to be bold

- It is a decision, a choice you have to make to be bold.

- You need to spend time with Jesus.

> Now when they saw the boldness of Peter and John, and perceived that they were unlearned and ignorant men, they marvelled; and they took knowledge of them, that they had been with Jesus.
> *Acts 4:13 (KJV)*

People who spend time with Jesus will be bold. Fear will be broken over their lives and they will move into a new dimension of boldness.

When faced with intimidation, combat it by walking in boldness. Sometimes, when I go somewhere to preach and stand in the pulpit, I can feel the spirit of intimidation in that place. I feel it trying to close me down. I will then take a few minutes to pray aloud and address the people in a bold way. As I do that the atmosphere changes, and I soon feel the release to preach.

3. Tenacity

The dictionary defines tenacious as:

> **Very determined or stubborn:** tending to stick firmly to any decision, plan, or opinion without changing, or doubting it
> **Tightly held:** difficult to loosen, shake off, or pull away from

Some in the Church today give up too quickly. They let go, and quit at the first or second opportunity. You will always have the opportunity to quit, but you must not take it. If the Lord has said something to you, then hold on to it despite what circumstances indicate or other people say. We need to be tenacious about our lives, families and our churches. We also need to be tenacious about our calling, and the mandate that has been given to us from the Lord. He would not call you to do something that you were unable to accomplish. He would not give you a charge, and then encourage you to stop halfway. Far too many people have let go of things when it became tough or the enemy applied pressure. It is time to pick up what the Lord gave you to walk in.

This end-time army will be tenacious; once they hold on to something, they will not let go until the required result has been achieved. They will have resolve in their eyes and steel in their backbones. The enemy will try everything to put them down or to cause them to let go of what the Lord told them, but to no avail.

A Canaanite woman from that vicinity came to him, crying out, 'Lord, Son of David, have mercy on me! My daughter is suffering terribly from demon-possession.' Jesus did not answer a word. So his disciples came to him and urged him, 'Send her away, for she keeps crying out after us.' He answered, 'I was sent only to the lost sheep of Israel.' The woman came and knelt before him. 'Lord, help me!' she said. He replied, 'It is not right to take the children's bread and toss it to their dogs.' 'Yes, Lord,' she said, 'but even the dogs eat the crumbs that fall from their masters' table.' Then Jesus answered, 'Woman, you have great faith! Your request is granted.' And her daughter was healed from that very hour.

Matthew 15:22-28 (NIV 1984)

This story is one of the best examples of tenacity in the Bible. A Canaanite woman came to Jesus asking for a miracle for her daughter. First, Jesus ignores her – but she keeps begging. Even when He tells her that He was only sent for the Israelites, she continues to beg. Jesus calls her a dog (in effect)! She could have been offended at this point. However, she says, 'You can call me what You like, but even the dogs get the crumbs!' It is then that Jesus grants her request.

What tenacity! With all that opposition and opportunities to let go and walk away, this woman held on to the hope that Jesus would heal her daughter. We need to learn from this story. It is not in the Bible accidentally, but for us to learn tenacity from it. Look with me at these words of Jesus below:

So I say to you: ask and it will be given to you; seek and you will find; knock and the door will be opened to you. For everyone who asks receives; the one who seeks finds; and to the one who knocks, the door will be opened.

Luke 11:9-10

Literally translated, the above is written in a continuous tense. Jesus is saying, 'Ask and keep on asking, seek and keep on seeking, knock and keep on knocking.' In other words, you must be tenacious if you are to get anything. Wishing for things, or praying once for things only half-heartedly is not enough. The trumpet is blowing raising men, women and children who will be tenacious in the way they live their lives and treat their destinies.

Tenacious in prayer

You will need to be tenacious in prayer. I have observed a growing tendency in churches – many Christians do not believe in the power of prayer. They see it only as a religious duty, not as a means of changing situations and circumstances. Through prayer, you can change anything. Nevertheless, it requires discipline and effort to keep coming into the place of consistent prayer. Tenacious prayers are so needed in the army today. The ability to hold on to an issue and pray day after day, month after month until we see the desired result – the old-time Pentecostals used to call it 'praying through'.

Tenacious in friendship

This is something that the Lord has really laid on my heart. Again, I have observed in church life how lightly many people treat friendships. People are easily offended and let go of friendships. I believe in these last days we must value friendships highly, and do our best to protect and cultivate them, so that they become all that God has ordained them to be. A loyalty and deep relational connections are coming into the body of Christ that have been lacking. A good example of this is seen in the relationship between Elijah and Elisha in 2 Kings 2. Elisha is the younger man, and has a friendship with Elijah. He knows that Elijah is about to be taken up to heaven, and he has three opportunities to leave him. Elijah tells him to stay behind, but Elisha chooses not to. Finally, he is granted his request for a double portion of Elijah's anointing.

He pursued this relationship, and it changed his life. It changed his life from the first time he met Elijah. However, Elisha had to pursue the relationship. Today in our churches, we must pursue friendship. God has divine relational connections that will take you to higher levels, but you must pursue the relationship for it to happen. Do not go for *any* friendship, but for God connections.

How to be tenacious

- You must make a choice: a choice not to let go of the things that you start to do.

- Ask for God's help to be tenacious.

- Make yourself accountable to someone whom you trust. Share your decision to become tenacious. Meet them regularly, and allow them to speak into your life and hold you accountable.

4. Militant

The dictionary defines militant as:

> **Aggressive:** extremely active in the defence or support of a cause, often in ways that other people find unacceptable
> **Involved in fighting:** engaged in fighting or warfare (spiritual)

'Militant' might not be the word you would use to describe the Church. But I believe that it is a godly characteristic, and one very much needed by the Church today. Our world is more militant today than ever before in films and advertising. I have observed the standard becoming lower and lower over the last ten years. As a family, choosing a film to watch has become more difficult. We have seen the rating of films become more and more relaxed. What would have been unacceptable ten years ago has become the norm.

We have seen an increasing rise of militant Islam over the last fifteen years, conflict in many part of the world, increasing terrorist attacks and much fear spread through beheadings, bombs and threats. Tens of thousands of people have been displaced.

There has been a clear and focused agenda which is at odds with traditional biblical marriage that has affected our society, schools, laws, employment, media and even the Church. It has been an unashamed drive to promote a lifestyle and society that is in stark opposition to the teaching of the Bible.

Our world has become an increasingly complex place to live, with tolerance and political correctness foremost in many people's thinking, living and planning. It is into this difficult and challenging situation that the Lord is asking His Church to be a strong, unapologetic but loving voice of truth. We are not militant against people. We are called to love people. But we must be active, unashamed and strong in our lives and witness for Christ. Our greatest weapons will be the fruit of the Holy Spirit: 'love, joy, peace, patience, kindness, goodness, faithfulness, gentleness and self-control' (Galatians 5:22-23, NIV 1984), and with these we will speak and live the truth without compromise.

> The LORD is a warrior; the LORD is his name.
> *Exodus 15:3*

This scripture tells us that God is a Warrior. That is a part of His nature and character that we are not too familiar with today, but I believe that it will be revealed to a greater degree in the coming days. It will be revealed through His body, the Church, the end-time army. We know His love, His grace, and even something of the fear of the Lord. These are all good, and we need to understand and know God through these revelations. However, there is coming a greater revelation of the Lord as a Warrior!

Militant in being a kingdom person

Jesus was a militant kingdom person; He spread the kingdom of God aggressively wherever He went. Lives were transformed, atmospheres changed and communities transformed. Paul the apostle was exactly the same. These men did not conform to their environment, but spread the hope, light and truth of the kingdom wherever they went. The kingdom inside Jesus, or Paul, invaded people's environment. It was militant; some found it offensive and extreme. Some rejected the men and the message; others found a life and hope that they had never known before. As an example of this, I see what the Message Trust are doing with schools work and their Eden projects as a clear, unapologetic advance of the gospel to those who need it most. They love people, but at the same time are unapologetic about the message of Christ.

Militant in our vision and planning

These Warriors will think outside the box. There will be no limitations upon them. They will see the world as a place that needs to be won for Jesus, and they will not be restricted by old methods of doing things – just like David when he tried on Saul's armour and answered:

> 'I cannot go in these,' he said to Saul, 'because I am not used to them.' So he took them off. Then he took his staff in his hand, chose five smooth stones from the stream, put them in the pouch of his shepherd's bag and, with his sling in his hand, approached the Philistine.
> *1 Samuel 17:39-40*

This army will not rely on past methods that may or may not have worked. They will not try to be fancy or clever. They are not here to impress someone or to look good, but to get the job done. They will go out in simplicity and purity with their faith in God. But they will be thinking advance. David wanted to fight Goliath, and remove him. He did not have some clever idea about running or hiding or distracting Goliath, but believed that God was big enough to deal with him. We too must be like David in this hour.

Think outside the box and allow the Holy Spirit to think through you. David was young and inexperienced and not the natural choice, but he was God's choice. God will give you ideas, vision and strategies that may not look good in the natural, but they will work because He gave them to you. Think different, think militant.

Militant in missions

> Then Jesus came to them and said, 'All authority in heaven and on earth has been given to me. Therefore go and make disciples of all nations, baptising them in the name of the Father and of the Son and of the Holy Spirit, and teaching them to obey everything I have commanded you. And surely I am with you always, to the very end of the age.'
> *Matthew 28:18-20*

When you read these words of Jesus, you see that the only way to obey them is by taking the good news into places that are hostile and possibly dangerous. You need to go into an area with the mentality of spiritual warfare. You need to replace the dominion of darkness with the kingdom of God. I believe that the Lord wants us to have great impact in our missions and advancement of the Great Commission. There are many who must be rescued from the dominion of darkness, and it will take an intentional obedience to the Great Commission in order to accomplish that. These missions must be combined with strong praying and clear, uncompromised preaching of the gospel.

Militant with a demonstration of the fruit of the Spirit

> But the fruit of the Spirit is love, joy, peace, patience, kindness, goodness, faithfulness, gentleness and self-control. Against such things there is no law. Those who belong to Christ Jesus have crucified the sinful nature with its passions and desires. Since we live by the Spirit, let us keep in step with the Spirit.

Let us not become conceited, provoking and envying
each other.
Galatians 5:22-26 (NIV 1984)

This might sound like a contradiction, but I believe that it
is one of the most powerful ways to demonstrate the
kingdom in a militant manner. Our world is so full of
hatred, anger, strife, jealousy, competitiveness, impatience
and so on. We see this demonstrated each day in our
offices, schools, workplaces and even our homes. Often
behind such outbursts there are spiritual forces that want
to bring strife, division and separation between people. As
kingdom people, we should be releasing the fruit of the
Spirit into this environment. In situations of anger, bring
peace; in situations of hate, bring love, and in situations of
selfishness, bring kindness.

You have the ability to disarm the enemy in any given
situation by responding to the negative with the fruit of the
positive – the fruit of the Spirit. The enemy will be
disarmed as kingdom forces of love, joy and peace
suddenly come into that situation. There is so much power
in this, if only it were practised by believers. I remember
once walking into a room where some harsh conversations
had just taken place. I could feel accusation and anger in
the air, as well as a strong tension. I walked in, smiled,
laughed about something, and just started to love people.
Within minutes the atmosphere had changed, and people
were talking to each other, and smiling. It really works.

How to be militant

- Like the other characteristics, you need to make a decision to walk and live militantly.

- Read through the Gospels and the Acts of the Apostles, and see how Jesus and the early believers lived. This will stir up your faith and open your eyes to see how militant they really were. You could read these books in a week or two. Follow their example and live out your faith as they lived out theirs.

Summary

I have covered four characteristics in this chapter – focus, boldness, tenacity and militancy. I have also given details on how you can begin to apply these to your life. It is important for this end-time army to be fully prepared and strong. I encourage you to work out the teaching in this chapter into your life. This will require a decision and then discipline.

Tenacious – very determined and stubborn, difficult to shake off

Thanksgiving – an appreciation or grateful acknowledgement of grace, favour or service

Perseverance – constant or steady persistence in a course of action or in pursuit of an aim, continuance in a state of grace leading finally to a state of glory

Chapter 8
Characteristics of the
End-Time Army – Part 2

1. Thankful

The dictionary defines thanks as:

> an expression of gratitude or appreciation for something.

This characteristic is so opposed to the culture of our time, where so many feel they are entitled to things and become demanding. People seem to be less thankful and grateful then ever. Always striving for more, for bigger, for better, and not content with what they have. They often see the negative in a situation, rather than the positive. There seems to be more focus on what they do not have, rather than on the abundance of what they do have. Sadly, this attitude has subtly crept into the lives of believers and churches. We often focus our attention on what we do not have, or focus it on the one negative in a situation, rather than on the many blessings and provisions of God. The result is people who are negative, critical and ungrateful.

I believe there is a forgotten power in thanksgiving that needs to be regained by this end-time army. An attitude of gratitude and thankfulness not only changes the way we feel, it also changes the environment around us. It can lift your spirit and the heaviness in any situation. When my children were younger I taught them to say thank you, and to appreciate the good things with which they are blessed. In the Church, we need to teach people and leaders alike how to say thank you, and to appreciate the provision of the Lord with His ongoing grace and mercy in our lives.

Paul and Silas in prison

One of my favourite examples of the power of thanksgiving is the story of Paul and Silas. It is such a powerful illustration of a good attitude and the tremendous power of God.

> The crowd joined in the attack against Paul and Silas, and the magistrates ordered them to be stripped and beaten with rods. After they had been severely flogged, they were thrown into prison, and the jailer was commanded to guard them carefully. When he received these orders, he put them in the inner cell and fastened their feet in the stocks. About midnight Paul and Silas were praying and singing hymns to God, and the other prisoners were listening to them. Suddenly there was such a violent earthquake that the foundations of the prison were

shaken. At once all the prison doors flew open, and everyone's chains came loose.

Acts 16:22-26

These men have had no formal charge brought against them. They have been publicly stripped, beaten, severely flogged and thrown into prison. They were missionaries bringing the good news of Jesus to the people. All they had done was cast a demon out of a young girl who had been bound perhaps for years. They had every reason to allow a bad attitude to come into their hearts. They could have blamed God, blamed each other and severed their friendship. Instead, we read that about midnight, the darkest hour, they are found praying and singing hymns to God. With all their troubles, they still had reason to praise and thank God for His goodness. They kept their hearts clean and pure with a right, godly attitude. I believe that God was so touched by their faith and thankfulness that He performed a powerful miracle for them by setting them free and saving many. There is tremendous power in thanksgiving.

Oh, how I wish we in the Church had this kind of attitude. There has been too much criticism and backbiting, too much knocking each other down and complaining. The army of Warriors that is being raised will be full of gratitude for the salvation and the grace of God at work in their lives. They will be overwhelmed with thankfulness that God would even use them in the smallest way for the advancement of the kingdom. They know where they came from and what they deserved, but God in His grace saved them.

We are commanded to be thankful

> And whatever you do, whether in word or deed, do it all in the name of the Lord Jesus, giving thanks to God the Father through him.
> *Colossians 3:17*

> Devote yourselves to prayer, being watchful and thankful.
> *Colossians 4:2*

> So then, just as you received Christ Jesus as Lord, continue to live your lives in him, rooted and built up in him, strengthened in the faith as you were taught, and overflowing with thankfulness.
> *Colossians 2:6-7*

Look at these passages of Scripture and see how strongly Paul urges us to be devoted to thankfulness and to overflow with thankfulness. The attitude of thankfulness is not an option, but a command from the Word of God for us. It is commanded because God not only wants His children to have good attitudes, but He knows that there is power to change their lives if they live in thankfulness.

In 2 Chronicles 20, King Jehoshaphat faced a very difficult situation. Three nations had formed a large army against him, and he had no natural hope of survival. It was a desperate situation with no way out. The whole of Judah came to God in prayer and fasting, asking Him to help. God told them they would not need to fight but that He was with them. King Jehoshaphat sent the worshippers out first; they praised God and thanked Him for who He was.

In other words, they were adoring and focusing on the greatness of God and His promise to be with them, not on the greatness of their problem. As they went out praising, God did a miracle – confusion came in to the camp of the enemy, and they destroyed each other.

Thankfulness has the power to change atmospheres, and to release the miraculous. It can lift your depression and lighten your burden. God has ordained that certain things will change only through thankfulness.

How to be thankful

- You need to choose to be thankful. It starts with that all-important decision.

- Learn to focus on your blessings. Every day thank God for His provision, for life and for food. There are so many things for which to thank the Lord. You will need to learn to develop the attitude of thankfulness.

- Also, make a point of thanking people for all that they do for you. We can often take people for granted, especially those who are closest to us. We need to value and honour people, and we do that with our words of thanks and appreciation.

2. Commitment

The dictionary defines commitment as:

Responsibility: something that takes up time or energy, especially an obligation
Loyalty: devotion or dedication to a cause, person, or relationship

Previously planned engagement: a planned arrangement or activity that cannot be avoided

Just like thankfulness, commitment seems to be in short supply. In my experience as a pastor working with people for two decades, I have been surprised to hear the reasoning why some people will walk away from a job, a university course and even a marriage. When I was younger it seemed that commitment to meet with God's people on a Sunday was high but I have seen both in our local church and in travelling and speaking to leaders that many attend church every other or even every third Sunday. I know that there are varied and many reasons for these things and I don't want to generalise, but the fact still remains – commitment is being challenged.

People seem to have a mentality that they are committed until things get difficult, or someone offends them, or until they are asked to do something that they do not want to, or it costs them too much.

In my years as a pastor, I have had a number of people come, at various times, to tell me how committed they were to the church, and to the vision that the Lord has given us. They would tell me of how the Lord had spoken to them that they were to stand with us. I felt so encouraged and uplifted, promises were made and hugs exchanged. I have been very surprised that many of these same people are no longer around us. They made a commitment; the Lord spoke to them about what they should do but, for whatever reason, they have gone. Maybe they were offended by something we said or did. Perhaps the vision was not happening fast enough or they just fancied a change. All I know is that they did not follow through with their commitment. It is a sobering observation of the Church today. Thankfully, I also observe many great people in the Church who are shining examples of commitment to God and His people. I am humbled by their service.

Ruth and Naomi

This story, from the book of Ruth, is a powerful example of commitment. Over a period of time, Naomi had seen her two sons and her husband die. She is now left with her daughters-in-law, Orpah and Ruth. She decides to return to her home country and people. She encourages both women to go back to their respective families to remarry, and start life over again. They both say that they are committed to her, and that they will stick with her. She again encourages them to leave. Orpah agrees, and returns to her family. Ruth, however, gives an amazing response.

> 'Don't urge me to leave you or to turn back from you. Where you go I will go, and where you stay I will stay. Your people will be my people and your God my God. Where you die I will die, and there I will be buried. May the LORD deal with me, be it ever so severely, if anything but death separates you and me.' When Naomi realised that Ruth was determined to go with her, she stopped urging her.
> *Ruth 1:16-18 (NIV 1984)*

Ruth is committed to Naomi and their relationship, and she vows that nothing but death will break that friendship. What a powerful commitment: 'I will go where you go, your God will be my God, and your people my people.' She even goes as far as to say that she will die in the same land as Naomi. In other words, 'I am committed to you even after you die.'

Jonathan and his armour-bearer

Another very powerful story is that of Jonathan and his armour-bearer. There are just the two of them, they have one sword between them, and they are at war with the Philistines. Jonathan tells his armour-bearer to accompany him as he goes to attack a Philistine outpost, in which about twenty armed men were on duty.

> Jonathan said to his young armour-bearer, 'Come, let's go over to the outpost of those uncircumcised men. Perhaps the LORD will act on our behalf. Nothing can hinder the LORD from saving, whether by many or by few.' 'Do all that you have in mind,' his armour-bearer said. 'Go ahead; I am with you heart and soul.'
> *1 Samuel 14:6-7*

Look at the commitment of his armour-bearer. He believed in Jonathan and his calling, and was willing to risk his life to help him to do what God had put in his heart. I believe that God is restoring commitment like this back to His Church and it will be a strong characteristic of the Warriors God is raising. The present condition of the Church will change, and there will be a sense of loyalty to one another that unbelievers, and even some Christians, will not understand. I can already see the seeds of it in the Church as I travel around the world.

Early believers

> They devoted themselves to the apostles' teaching and to fellowship, to the breaking of bread and to prayer. Everyone was filled with awe at the many wonders and signs performed by the apostles. All the believers were together and had everything in common. They sold property and possessions to give to anyone who had need. Every day they continued to meet together in the temple courts. They broke bread in their homes and ate together with glad and sincere hearts, praising God and enjoying the favour of all the people. And the Lord added to their number daily those who were being saved.
>
> *Acts 2:42-47*

In this passage, we see the commitment of the Early Church. First, they were committed to the Lord, His calling upon their lives and their relationship with Him. This too must be our first place of commitment. This is where it starts; we need to be loyal to the Lord Jesus. It is so easy to speak words of commitment at services, or at times when we are emotionally moved, but then to forget or choose not follow through. In Ecclesiastes 5:4, we are told not to delay in fulfilling our vows to the Lord.

Second, we see their commitment to the apostles and their teaching. The devil has worked hard at trying to undermine leaders. Sometimes, as leaders, we have been our own worst enemies by the way we have behaved. Sadly, in some places, the relationship between people and leaders has suffered, so that it becomes more formal than relational. I believe that this must change, and indeed, is changing. God has ordained leaders, and He chooses to operate His kingdom through them. He will show things to leaders that others may not see. He chooses to govern His people through leaders. Yet today, so many think that they do not need a pastor or leaders. They think that they know it all themselves, and that their relationship with God is enough to get them to their destination. If we did not need leaders, God would not have put them in place in His body. Leaders lead the people by guiding them, governing them, helping them to discover their destiny and enabling them to walk in it, and God has given us elders, deacons[13] and the fivefold ministry gifts too.[14]

There needs to be a fresh commitment from leaders to the people, and from the people to the leaders. The blame for our present condition lies both with leaders and with the people. We have too many leaders who have hurt people and abused them. We have also had many people that have hurt leaders and abused them. It is time to grow up, and allow God to bring us into a right relationship. There is much power in the commitment between these two.

Last, but not least, we need to be committed to each other. I believe that as we get the first two right this one will fall into place. So many attend church today but do not really build strong, committed relationships. Christians attend church and think that is enough, but we were not commanded to attend a church building, but to be family – brothers, sisters, mothers and fathers. We are supposed to

---

[13] 1 Timothy 3:1-13.
[14] Ephesians 4:11-12.

be family, but family in our world has been destroyed and broken up. We need to show the world what true family looks like, and allow God to restore what has been broken.

I believe that when this type of commitment and loyalty comes into the Church we will be irresistible to the world. They will look at us and want to be a part of such a close family. People are longing for relationships where they can find true commitment and loyalty. It is essential for this end-time army to have this as a characteristic, if they are to walk in the fullness of their mandate from God.

How to be committed

- It will start with a decision that you need to make – to stop running from problems and relationships, and to be committed.

- Talk to people you trust, and share with them that you would like to be more committed. Allow them to speak into your life to help bring accountability.

- Regularly evaluate your life to see if you have stayed committed in situations and relationships. Do not make excuses, but be honest with yourself and learn.

3. Perseverance

The dictionary defines perseverance as:

> a determined continuation with something: steady and continued action or belief, usually over a long period despite difficulties or setbacks

Therefore, since we are surrounded by such a great cloud of witnesses, let us throw off everything that hinders and the sin that so easily entangles. And let us run with perseverance the race marked out for us.
Hebrews 12:1

There is a race marked out for each person, and it is not a short, fast race, but a long endurance race. It is not too important how you start, but that you complete the race that has been set for you to run. For you to do this effectively, you must have the characteristic of perseverance – that is, an ability to keep on keeping on despite setbacks or difficulties. You do not have to be the fastest or strongest, but you have to keep going. You may not be the most gifted or anointed, but you know how to persevere in something.

I have recently observed that many of the heroes I look up to in the Christian world are, in reality, no more gifted than others. In fact, some seem to have less gifting. But they have that ability to persevere, to keep doing what God has called them to do. They go through setbacks and crisis, but they just keep running. I believe that God sees this, and grants these people greater influence and fruitfulness.

Persevere in your calling

There are many destinies abandoned by the roadside. People gave up because of the negative words of others, or maybe they experienced setback and delay. If you have done that with your calling, you need to pick it up today, and make up your mind that you are going to persevere in your calling, and start to run with it again. Between your promise and the Promised Land there is always a wilderness of the exact opposite. And it's normally in that wilderness that our character is developed. Understanding this has helped me to persevere through the wilderness.

Persevere in your relationship with the Lord

Far too many have settled in a place of mediocrity and complacency with the Lord. You can make your relationship with God as deep and as intimate as you want to. You do not have to settle where you are today. I believe that God wants His children to persevere in their relationship with Him. I often say to my wife, 'Why can't we have the best marriage on earth?' I am not being proud in this statement, but encouraging us both to reach for more, to persevere and not quit. We need to do the same with our relationship with the Lord. It is from this one relationship that the success of all you have and do will come. Persevere in it.

Persevere in your relationship with each other

We are told in Psalm 133 that where brothers dwell together in unity God commands a blessing. We need to persevere with each other, not quit and simply walk away. When dealing with people, there will always be the opportunity for offence and misunderstanding. We must not take these opportunities, but persevere in our friendship with those whom God has put into our lives. I am not saying here that it is OK for people to mistreat you and waste your time, and that you have to put up with it. There must be honesty, openness and rebuke where necessary, but do not give up on the person.

Consider him who endured such opposition from sinners, so that you will not grow weary and lose heart.
Hebrews 12:3

Dear friends, do not be surprised at the painful trial you are suffering, as though something strange were happening to you. But rejoice that you participate in the sufferings of Christ, so that you may be overjoyed when his glory is revealed.
1 Peter 4:12-13 (NIV 1984)

Let Jesus be your example. He persevered with people and situations because He knew the end goal was worth it. Keep the end in mind, the prize, and allow it to give you the strength to persevere. One of the keys to persevering in my calling or with relationships is that I can see what they will become. I see the end goal and it drives me to keep going. Persevere.

4. Humility

The dictionary regards humility as:

> connected to the word 'humus' (Greek) which means ground, earthy, agreeing with the truth

Pride comes before a fall. We know that is what happened to Lucifer (see Isaiah 14; Ezekiel 28). Pride caused him to be cast down from heaven. He was exalted in his own mind, and began to think too highly of himself. We must be careful in these days to make sure that we guard against this very powerful strategy of the enemy. It is very easy to fall to pride, but once we do, it becomes very difficult to see clearly. The enemy then uses this opportunity to attack us. The only way to fight pride is to be clothed with humility.

> When pride comes, then comes disgrace, but with humility comes wisdom.
> *Proverbs 11:2*

Humility is simply agreeing with the truth. There are two extremes, and truth is in the middle. Some think more highly of themselves than they ought, and hence exceed the truth. Others think less of themselves than they should, and thus fall short of the truth. The first one we recognise as pride, but the second one is also pride – in the form of false humility. The place of humility is the place where we agree with the truth. We must choose to live in that place.

Think too highly

> On the appointed day Herod, wearing his royal robes, sat on his throne and delivered a public address to the people. They shouted, 'This is the voice of a god, not of a man.' Immediately, because Herod did not give praise to God, an angel of the Lord struck him down, and he was eaten by worms and died.
> *Acts 12:21-23*

Herod believed what the people said, and had a more exalted opinion of himself than was actually true. Sadly, I see that this is so common in the Church and world today, both with ministers and the people. God uses people. Some of them then think that they are great, and should be worshipped. I have seen people in the Church who walk around and talk with such pride. They believe that they are more important than others, and that they should be consulted for advice. They begin to believe that it is difficult for them to make mistakes, and soon stop listening to those around them. They begin to pass judgement on others, and think they are hearing from the Lord. The truth is that they are often listening to the accusations and lies of the enemy and then repeating them.

Sadly, I have seen these people taken in by pride, and the enemy begins to destroy their lives. The Lord is gracious, and gives them many opportunities to repent, but some refuse. They live in a place of deception. When things start to go wrong, they have spiritual answers prepared and ready. The sad thing is they actually begin to believe these lies.

> Do not let anyone who delights in false humility and the worship of angels disqualify you for the prize. Such a person goes into great detail about what he has seen, and his unspiritual mind puffs him up with idle notions.
> *Colossians 2:18 (NIV 1984)*

As ministers, we too need to be very careful that we do not fall into the trap of pride. For those who are often in the public eye, it is easy to start believing your own publicity, and to think that you really are something fantastic. Remember where you have come from and who brought you to where you are today. It is only the grace of God that could have done what has been done in your life. Make it a daily habit to remind yourself of God's goodness and grace. Surround yourself with people who are not afraid to speak the truth to you and give them permission to speak into your life. I have said to many around me that if they see me going towards error in any way, they have a duty to speak to me about it. Those kinds of relationships will keep you strong for the long haul.

> The fear of the LORD teaches a man wisdom, and humility comes before honour.
> Proverbs 15:33 (NIV 1984)

False humility

False humility is as real a problem today as thinking too highly of oneself. In fact, it may even be a greater problem to many. People play down the truth, and want to be seen as humble, but that too is pride and it is very dangerous. Both forms of pride will blind you, and give room for the enemy to attack. You must learn to agree with the truth. If someone gives you a compliment for something that you have done, learn to accept it, and say thank you. I often say, 'Thank you for your encouragement. I appreciate it.' It would be wrong of me to say, 'It was nothing. It was all the Lord.' I once remember hearing the story of a young lady who was complimented for her singing and she replied, 'It was all the Lord.' The man who had complimented her turned to her and said, 'It wasn't that good. I am sure the Lord could have done better.' Though this is humorous, there is truth in it.

The key is simply to agree with the truth, and not to exceed it. You have a choice to humble yourself or to be humbled. It is much easier to humble oneself than to be humbled.

> Seek the LORD, all you humble of the land, you who do what he commands. Seek righteousness, seek humility; perhaps you will be sheltered on the day of the LORD'S anger.
> *Zephaniah 2:3*

> Therefore, as God's chosen people, holy and dearly loved, clothe yourselves with compassion, kindness, humility, gentleness and patience.
> *Colossians 3:12*

How to be humble

- Remind yourself of where you have come from and the goodness of the Lord to you. Rehearse His goodness and grace by praying, thanking and even regularly talking to others about how gracious God is.

- Ask the Holy Spirit to help you stay humble, and not to fall into pride. Make this a daily prayer. You may find yourself praying this prayer a number of times a day.

5. Love

I believe that the best definition of love is found in 1 Corinthians 13:4-8:

Love is patient, love is kind. It does not envy, it does not boast, it is not proud. It is not rude, it is not self-seeking, it is not easily angered, it keeps no record of wrongs. Love does not delight in evil but rejoices with the truth. It always protects, always trusts, always hopes, always perseveres. Love never fails.
1 Corinthians 13:4-8 (NIV 1984)

When Jesus was asked by a religious teacher what the most important commandment was, this was His reply:

'Love the Lord your God with all your heart and with all your soul and with all your mind.' This is the first and greatest commandment. And the second is like it: 'Love your neighbour as yourself.' All the Law and the Prophets hang on these two commandments.
Matthew 22:37-40

The greatest command is first to love God and second, to love people. Love is at the core of the gospel. John 3:16 tells us that it was because God so loved this world that He sent His Son to die for it. He was not motivated out of religious duty, or an obligation to the human race. He was motivated by love. We too need to understand the importance of love in all we do. All that we do and all that we are must be driven by love for God and love for people.

The apostle Paul tells us that it is the love of God that compels him to preach the gospel of Jesus Christ. He teaches us in the famous 'love chapter' of 1 Corinthians 13 that without love you fail, and all your work is useless.

If I speak in the tongues of men or of angels, but do not have love, I am only a resounding gong or a clanging cymbal. If I have the gift of prophecy and can fathom all mysteries and all knowledge, and if I have a faith that can move mountains, but do not have love, I am nothing. If I give all I possess to the poor and give over my body to hardship that I may boast, but do not have love, I gain nothing.
1 Corinthians 13:1-3

These are very powerful, potent words. We cannot ignore them. This end-time army must be driven by and clothed in love; love for God, love for each other, and love for the lost of this world. The apostle Paul says in verse 8 that 'love never fails'. It is the one thing that will not fail. I think we would be surprised if we could see how the love-walk is connected to so many areas in our lives. The answer to your situation may be as simple as walking in love. For example, you may believe God for a particular matter and be exercising your faith, yet you have not seen the results. This scripture tells us that faith works through love.

For in Jesus Christ neither circumcision availeth any thing, nor uncircumcision; but faith which worketh by love.
Galatians 5:6 (KJV)

A preacher friend of mine told me a story about a lady who had been heavily involved in witchcraft, and was seeking to be free from these tormenting spirits. She had turned up at a Christian Bible week, and was looking for help. A few believers had tried to help her, but they only seemed to aggravate the spirits within her rather than cast them out. My friend simply spoke a word to her, he cast them out and she was freed. There were no great manifestations or struggles as there had been previously. They were gone with a word. She later commented that the reason he was able to do this was because his prayer had been motivated by love. Those who had prayed for her before were looking for a trophy or a great demonstration, but were unconcerned about the lady. She told him not to underestimate the power of love. 'Love never fails.' We must make the love walk a strong part of our Christian life.

I believe that this is the greatest characteristic for this end-time army to have. You will see it in their eyes, and it will be demonstrated in their life and actions. Many of the other characteristics that I have mentioned are strongly connected to this one. If you make this one the priority, it will help you in fulfilling the others. Remember: 'Love never fails.'

How to walk in love

- It is a choice, but a disciplined choice. Once you make this decision, the enemy will throw everything at you to stop you walking in love. Nevertheless, you can walk in love because Romans 5:5 tells us that the love of God has been poured into our hearts.

Summary

We have looked at these five characteristics:

- Thankfulness;

- Commitment;

- Perseverance;
- Humility;
- Love.

As these are applied to your life, they will help you to achieve your full potential in Christ. They will enable you to be a blessing, and to help other members of the army. *You* must decide to bring them into your life, and then start the process to do that.

Community – the condition of sharing or having certain attitudes and interests in common

Leadership – the action of leading a group of people or an organisation

Accountable – responsible to someone, able to be called to account for actions

Chapter 9
Assembled and in Order

Come quickly, all you nations from every side, and assemble there. Bring down your warriors, LORD!
Joel 3:11 (my emphasis)

I think it is interesting to note from this passage that the army is not only being roused to action, but that these Warriors are being called to come and assemble. This is a call for every Warrior to be in his or her right place within the army. It speaks of order and rank within the army, no pushing or shoving. No one is trying to take another person's place. There is a correct understanding of authority and rank. The Warriors are submitted and accountable. This is very important in these end days. This end-time army must move as a unit, a body. We can only do that when we find our rightful place and operate in it, and when we value and appreciate the other parts of the body. It is important to understand that we all need each other to complete the task that has been given to us. It is also important to discover our unique gifts and skills, and much of this process happens by walking the Christian life with others and allowing them to help us to see ourselves better.

Authentic community

> They devoted themselves to the apostles' teaching and to fellowship, to the breaking of bread and to prayer. Everyone was filled with awe at the many wonders and signs performed by the apostles. All the believers were together and had everything in common. They sold property and possessions to give to anyone who had need. Every day they continued to meet together in the temple courts. They broke bread in their homes and ate together with glad and sincere hearts, praising God and enjoying the favour of all the people. And the Lord added to their number daily those who were being saved.
> *Acts 2:42-47*

This description of the Early Church is a beautiful picture of authentic community working well. Not without its problems, but still a powerful and glorious way of building New Testament family. There is a commitment to the leaders that God has placed to help serve, teach and grow the believers. There is true fellowship, and Spirit-empowered serving taking place among them all. We see the miraculous is commonplace, the cross is central and people are committed to this deep relational way of living out their faith in Christ. And many new people are turning to Christ each day.

I believe this is being restored to the body of Christ in our day. It has been one of my longings to see true fellowship in the Church, empowered by the Holy Spirit and forming strong joining within His body. I have observed over the last twenty-five years that we in the West struggle with wanting to privatise our faith. I have heard people tell me, 'It's my relationship with God; He speaks to me. I can hear Him.' What they are really saying is, 'I don't need others.' I have heard some people say that they do not need to be committed in a single local church because they have everything they need. But this flies in opposition to the New Testament's teaching and what we read of how the Early Church lived. They knew their faith was a communal thing and they needed others who were in the body of Christ.

Being planted

> They will be called oaks of righteousness, a planting
> of the LORD for the display of his splendour.
> *Isaiah 61:3b*

I believe the Lord plants us within church communities, and we are both blessed by bringing our gifts, talents and personality into that community. And we are blessed because of the others who are there that will enrich our lives and help us to live better for Jesus. Christian life is meant to be lived out in community. Our kingdom is primarily about relationship: relationship with God, relationship with each other and, finally, relationship with the world we are to reach. So we must not reduce it simply to attending somewhere on a Sunday or listening to some teaching for our own personal growth. Please allow me to challenge those who have had a habit of going from church to church to settle down in one place and build deep, meaningful relationships. Other people need you and you also need them. And for those who are committed to a church but have not built meaningful Christ-centred relationships, let me encourage you to join a house group (perhaps called a life or home group), if your church runs them, or to seek out some people to build relationship with.

We need leaders

> It was he who gave some to be apostles, some to be prophets, some to be evangelists, and some to be pastors and teachers, to prepare God's people for works of service, so that the body of Christ may be built up until we all reach unity in the faith and in the knowledge of the Son of God and become mature, attaining to the whole measure of the fullness of Christ.
> *Ephesians 4:11-13 (NIV 1984)*

God has given leaders to the Church to prepare people for 'works of service', and to bring them into a place of maturity. The Holy Spirit is challenging both leaders and people that we may value, love and serve each other so that God's will and ways would come on earth. The leader's role is to help people grow into a place of maturity where they will fulfil their destiny. And I believe the people should be willing and committed to what the Lord is calling the Church to. A lot of time has been lost with infighting, misunderstanding and the like.

A word to leaders

God has set leaders over His people to serve the people and help to bring them into the Promised Land. The people whom God has entrusted to you are not there to make you feel good, or even to serve you. Ultimately, they are God's people, and they have been entrusted to you. Take care of them, prepare and release them into ministry. Ephesians 4 is clear that the role of leaders is to prepare the people for 'works of service'. The people are the real ministers. This may come as shock, but you are there to release them into ministry. This may not be full-time ministry, but your church will do the real work when it goes out into the community. We have our thinking wrong if we believe that the real work is in a Sunday meeting. The kingdom and the Church would grow very fast if your church people operated as workers for the kingdom every day. If you are reading this as a leader, then I urge you to take these thoughts to the Lord in prayer.

I do believe that people should honour and serve their leaders. This is good, and is needed in today's Church. Leaders too must understand what the Lord has given them to do. I believe that God will not take kindly to His people being mistreated. They are ultimately *His* people. We are told in the Word that we, as leaders who teach, 'will be judged more strictly' (James 3:1). I encourage you to love and serve the people. You must desire and work hard to help fulfil their dreams and potential.

A word to the people

Leaders may have hurt you in the past, but you must allow God to heal you from that hurt, and to bring you into a place of wholeness. He can restore you and your faith in His leaders. Leaders have hurt me in the past. I have been overlooked and mistreated. I had to be careful to keep my heart clean, and not to allow bitterness to come in. In our world, a few bad doctors have mistreated their patients. However, most of us still go to our doctor and trust him. One bad doctor does not make all doctors bad. It is the same with leaders.

I encourage you to think that you are not in church just to attend services. You are there to be equipped for your everyday life so that you can minister for Jesus in the workplace and the marketplace. Church is a place to which we come to be refreshed, taught and empowered, so that we can take our place in Christ's body, and live our lives as true Christians. Church should be family, and we need to love and support one another. Go with joy and expectancy, and get involved in church life to serve other brothers and sisters. Choose to invite people into your life and live interdependent.

I also believe that we need to learn to submit to our leaders and honour them. God has blessed us with leaders, and we need to accept them as a blessing from God. They are a gift from God to help us mature and reach our potential. Honour the gift in them, and receive your leaders well. Honouring is done in the way you speak. Learn to speak well of your leaders and to lift them up in your conversations; pray for them. Do not knock them down.

You also honour them by obeying what they teach from Scripture, and being committed to the vision the Lord has given them.

Finding your place

Some people do not want to be where they have been placed; they desire another's job. They manipulate and control to try to get there. I have seen this happen with people in church life. Some will hand out their business cards to promote themselves and get to another place. Others will keep talking about how spiritual they are, and what God is doing through them or speaking to them. They are trying in their flesh to get to another place other than where God has put them. God promotes. God puts people where He wants them to be. If you get somewhere by your own efforts, then you will have to maintain your hard efforts and struggles to stay there. If God puts you there, then He will keep you there, and no one can remove you from that place.

> Then the king [David] said to Zadok, 'Take the ark of God back into the city. If I find favour in the LORD'S eyes, he will bring me back and let me see it and his dwelling-place again. But if he says, "I am not pleased with you," then I am ready; let him do to me whatever seems good to him.'
> *2 Samuel 15:25-26*

David understood this principle when his son Absalom tried to take the throne from him (2 Samuel 15). David did not try to struggle and hold on to power, but kept his faith in God. He knew that no one could remove him from where God had placed him, other than God Himself. Absalom was killed and David remained in power. God is big enough to move you to where He wants you to be. He knows the desires in your heart, but He also knows what you are ready for. He is the same God who found David as a shepherd boy and brought him into kingship. He can find you. Do not get upset and struggle with people, but take it to the Lord, and you will see that He directs things.

Faithfulness brings greater responsibility

> His master replied, 'Well done, good and faithful servant! You have been faithful with a few things; I will put you in charge of many things. Come and share your master's happiness!'
> *Matthew 25:23*

I advise you to be faithful where God has put you. The key is faithfulness. Faithfulness in small things will bring increased opportunities. The way up is down. The greatest in the kingdom is the servant. God is looking for faithful servants whom He can trust to do the tasks that no one else wants to do. Do the things that have no glory attached to them, and watch God put you where He can use you best. When you read the lives of Joseph, David and Daniel, you will find one major characteristic in their success. They were faithful wherever they were put. David looked after sheep faithfully, so God made him king. Joseph looked after Potiphar's house and the prison before he was given the palace. Daniel was faithful to God in his lifestyle and holiness even though he was in a foreign country, and God promoted him to be one of the top leaders in the land.

> And the things that thou hast heard of me among many witnesses, the same commit thou to faithful men, who shall be able to teach others also.
> *2 Timothy 2:2 (KJV)*

The apostle Paul tells Timothy, 'When you're looking for leaders and preachers, look for faithful men.' You must be faithful in managing yourself and your relationship with the Lord. Be faithful in your job, and be trustworthy. Show faithfulness in looking after your family. The Bible tells us that it starts at home (see 1 Timothy 5:8). Be faithful in your commitment to the church. God looks for the faithful. So many have a vision of great things that they want to do for the Lord, but they cannot turn up to church on time, or they struggle to stay in their job and be faithful there.

Honouring one another

> But in fact God has arranged the parts in the body, every one of them, just as he wanted them to be.
> *1 Corinthians 12:18 (NIV 1984)*

> Be devoted to one another in love. Honour one another above yourselves.
> *Romans 12:10*

> Do nothing out of selfish ambition or vain conceit, but in humility consider others better than

> yourselves. Each of you should look not only to your
> own interests, but also to the interests of others.
> *Philippians 2:3-4 (NIV 1984)*

These words of Paul are so strong and they are a tremendous challenge to us. The end-time Warriors must value and honour each other. We must recognise the importance and worth of each member of the body, and then learn to be devoted to them. In 1 Corinthians 12, Paul tells us that we are all made up of different parts, but we are one body. Without the different parts, the body would not be complete. Each member of the body is important and is needed for the body to function properly.

The Church is not supposed to be just a group of people who believe the same thing. It is not a social club. We are a family committed to one another, understanding that we need each other. We need to prefer each other and honour each other. I believe that a church with these characteristics will attract people very easily. Let us learn to honour the stranger in our midst, the young and the elderly. In fact, everyone who comes into contact with us should feel honoured for having done so. However, it will start with looking out for each other. Galatians 6:10 tells us to do good to everyone, but 'especially to those who are of the household of faith' (NKJV).

Conclusion

If the end-time army does not assemble correctly in unity with rank and order, we will end up with chaos and confusion. It is essential for us in the end time to obey the teaching of the Bible, to love, serve and honour each other.

As with everything in the Christian life, these truths will start with a decision, and then the patience to work them out over a long period. Not everything will change overnight, but we must start the journey.

Application

It is so important for this end-time army to be assembled and in order. There is a need for each person to be in their correct place, fulfilling their God-given destiny.

- What things do you need to do in order to move into the right place?

- No matter how difficult it might be, if there are wrongs that need to be put right, make a choice to do it.

- If you ask God, He will give you the grace to do these things.

Return – come or go back to a place

Urgency – immediate need for action: the fact or state of requiring immediate action, immediate attention or speed

Watch – an act or instance of carefully observing someone or something over a period of time

Chapter 10
Ready or Not, Here He Comes

'Men of Galilee,' they said, 'why do you stand here looking into the sky? This same Jesus, who has been taken from you into heaven, will come back in the same way you have seen him go into heaven.'
Acts 1:11

We know that Jesus Christ has promised that He would return. We call this the second coming of Christ. In today's Church it doesn't get mentioned a whole lot, but in the Early Church and in Church history it is a core theme and expectation of Christ-followers. It shaped the way they lived their lives, the way they preached and the urgency with which they spoke to non-believers. There are a number of opinions about how and when Christ will return, and though I am studying and growing in wisdom on the subject, I don't wish to go into details about every aspect here. But where I would like to focus our attention is that Jesus Christ will return, His coming is close; we must be ready for His return and we must live in the light of eternity.

Sign of the times

> No one knows about that day or hour, not even the angels in heaven, nor the Son, but only the Father.
> *Matthew 24:36 (NIV 1984)*

However, no one but the Father knows the day or the hour that He will return. We are told that it will happen suddenly, and without warning (see 1 Thessalonians 5:2), but no time or date is given to us. But even though a specific date is not given, signs of the times are, and remember – signs point to something. In Matthew 24 Jesus lists a number of signs. Here are a few of them, found in verses 4-14:

- 'Watch out that no one deceives you.

- … many will come in my name, claiming, "I am the Messiah," and will deceive many.

- You will hear of wars and rumours of wars, but see to it that you are not alarmed. Such things must happen, but the end is still to come.

- Nation will rise against nation,

- … kingdom against kingdom.

- There will be famines and earthquakes in various places.

- All these are the beginning of birth-pains.

- Then you will be handed over to be persecuted and put to death, and you will be hated by all nations because of me.

- At that time many will turn away from the faith and will betray and hate each other,

- ... many false prophets will appear and deceive many people.

- Because of the increase of wickedness, the love of most will grow cold,

- but the one who stands firm to the end will be saved.

- And this gospel of the kingdom will be preached in the whole world as a testimony to all nations,

- ... then the end will come ...'

For 2,000 years these things have been taking place around the world, but there seems to be an increase in frequency and intensity of these 'birth-pangs', as Jesus calls them.

We could list the signs over the last fifteen to twenty years. But it would take too long and not serve my purpose for this chapter. But enough to say that there has been an increase in wars and rumours of wars, especially what we see escalating in the Middle East, North Korea and with the way Russia has been and is manoeuvering itself. When Jesus said 'nation will rise against nation', the original language is 'ethnos' or ethnic group against ethnic group. We have seen an increase in racial violence in the last few years in America, Britain and Syria and in places in Africa too. Tsunamis, earthquakes, wild fires and famine – it seems as if they are almost daily news, so much so that we can easily become desensitised. But we must stay alert and pay attention to the signs of the times. Jesus also prophesied that the love of many Christians would grow cold as wickedness increases; does this describe the Church today? How in love with Jesus and each other are we?

Watch – be alert

> Therefore keep watch, because you do not know on
> what day your Lord will come.
> *Matthew 24:42*

The challenge that we are left with throughout Matthew 24 is to make sure that we will be ready for that return when it happens. Jesus stressed that the second coming will happen without warning, and that we must ensure that we are not living carelessly. This means we live in a state of readiness and expectations for Christ's return. This means we take His commands with soberness, we live our lives in the light of His return and that we embrace his mission with urgency to see His kingdom come and His will be done.

We will give an account

> So then, each of us will give an account of ourselves
> to God.
> *Romans 14:12*

> But I tell you that everyone will have to give account
> on the day of judgment for every empty word they
> have spoken.
> *Matthew 12:36*

Many Christians live their lives oblivious of the fact that each of us will one day give an account for the way we have lived. We will have to give an account of all that was entrusted to us. We really have and own nothing, but are simply stewards of everything. The time we have been given, the relationships, money, gifts and talents, everything is to be stewarded for God's glory. It all belongs to Him and one day He will ask us how we used it. I fear that many on that day will be embarrassed and ashamed that they used those things simply and mostly for themselves. Living in the light of eternity means that I ask myself how my choices, words, spending will look in the light of eternity. Instead of having a forty-year view of life, having a 400-year view. This simple but profound perspective would change much about the way we behave, our relationships and values.

Dark and light

> Arise, shine, for your light has come, and the glory
> of the LORD rises upon you. See, darkness covers the
> earth and thick darkness is over the peoples, but the
> LORD rises upon you and his glory appears over you.
> *Isaiah 60:1-2*

I believe this Old Testament scripture is prophesying about our day. We are called to arise and shine because God's glory rises upon us. In other words, change posture and burn brightly, radiate His life, goodness and hope to the world around you. Isaiah acknowledges that darkness is covering the earth and thick darkness the people, but that God's glory appears over you. I am convinced that this will be the finest hour for the Church. There will be a rise in both darkness and glory – God's activity through the Church on the earth. There will be a clash of kingdoms and the greatest harvest of souls is yet to be brought into the kingdom of God. These will not be easy or comfortable days but they will be glorious, especially for those who give ear to what the Spirit is saying to the Church and respond with quick and full obedience. We don't need to be in fear but we do need to be sober, looking to Christ and living fully for Him.

Urgent action required

> Be very careful, then, how you live – not as unwise
> but as wise, making the most of every opportunity,
> because the days are evil.
> *Ephesians 5:15-16*

Please take the scripture above very seriously. There is a need for urgency in this hour. The Lord is requiring us to obey Him quickly and fully. It is time to arise and take our rightful place. We need to seize every opportunity that He gives us, and make the most of it, squeezing all we can out of it. We cannot afford to miss whatever He sends our way. Value each open door and every relationship, and make the most of them. Every day is full of opportunity. Even in the mundane we can see Lord working His purposes.

And do this, understanding the present time: the hour has already come for you to wake up from your slumber, because our salvation is nearer now than when we first believed. The night is nearly over; the day is almost here. So let us put aside the deeds of darkness and put on the armour of light. Let us behave decently, as in the daytime, not in carousing and drunkenness, not in sexual immorality and debauchery, not in dissension and jealousy. Rather, clothe yourselves with the Lord Jesus Christ, and do not think about how to gratify the desires of the flesh.

Romans 13:11-14

It is time to wake out of slumber, out of apathy and out of lukewarmness into a place of being fiery hot and a blazing light for Jesus. We are the light and salt of the earth (see Matthew 5:13-16). We have the living God inside us and have been entrusted with the greatest truth and message ever. Let us put aside all that would slow us down and 'run with perseverance the race marked out for us' (Hebrews 12:1). Learn to live with eternity in view.

Only one life,
Twill soon be past
Only what's done
For Christ will last

Thank you for reading this book. I trust that it has challenged you. Now that you have finished it, the real work of putting it into practice starts. Do not let this be another book that you put down and think, 'well, that was good', but then do nothing to change your lifestyle. My prayer is that you are stirred to action.

> Do not merely listen to the word, and so deceive yourselves. Do what it says.
> *James 1:22*

Hearing the Word and not doing it leads the believer into deception. Sadly, many believers are in very strong deception because they have heard so very much and done so very little. We think that it is enough to hear or read a message, and understand it. God is looking for changed lives, not just hearers. I encourage you to reread the challenge of the first chapter and then obey.

THE TRUMPET HAS SOUNDED ... THE WARRIORS
HAVE BEEN SUMMONED ...
WILL YOU BE ONE OF THEM?

Contact details

Visit the All Nations Church website at:

www.allnations.org.uk

or email info@allnations.org.uk

You can also visit www.steveuppal.com

You will find more information about what we do, as well as sermons that you can download.

All Nations Church
Temple Street
Wolverhampton
WV2 4AQ

Tel: 01902 714469